D1460555

9030 00008 0113 9

KNEAD PEACE

KYLE BOOKS

KNEAD PEACE

'Baking connects good people and lets them understand
each other no matter what language they speak.'
—Anna Makievska, The Bakehouse, Kyiv

An Hachette UK Company
www.hachette.co.uk

First published in Great Britain
in 2022 by Kyle Books, an imprint
of Octopus Publishing Group Limited
Carmelite House
50 Victoria Embankment
London EC4Y 0DZ
www.kylebooks.co.uk

ISBN: 978 1 80419 075 3

Design and layout copyright © Octopus
Publishing Group Limited 2022
Text and image copyright see page 187

Distributed in the US by Hachette Book
Group, 1290 Avenue of the Americas, 4th
and 5th Floors, New York, NY 10104

Distributed in Canada by Canadian Manda
Group, 664 Annette St., Toronto, Ontario,
Canada M6S 2C8

Andrew Green is hereby identified as the author
of this work in accordance with section 77 of
the Copyright, Designs and Patents Act 1988.

All rights reserved. No part of this work may
be reproduced or utilised in any form or by
any means, electronic or mechanical, including
photocopying, recording or by any information
storage and retrieval system, without the
prior written permission of the publisher.

Publishing Director: Judith Hannam
Publisher: Joanna Copestick
Editor: Isabel Jessop
Copyeditor: Claire Rogers
Interior Design: Kate Thomas Wood
Cover Design: Jonathan Christie
Photography: Jessica Wang
Illustrations: Jessica Gully, @jessmotif
Production: Katherine Hockley

Printed and bound in Europe

10 9 8 7 6 5 4 3 2 1

MIX
Paper | Supporting
responsible forestry
FSC   FSC® C015829
www.fsc.org

LONDON BOROUGH OF WANDSWORTH	
9030 00008 0113 9	
Askews & Holts	
641.815	
	WW22009011

CONTENTS

Bread baking has always been an act of creation for me. And I hadn't considered myself a creator before I baked my first sourdough bread with the formula I made. Actually, this particular bread recipe you will find in the book (see pages 19–21). The bakery I co-founded and named The Bakehouse is the artisan bakery in Kyiv, Ukraine. We have baked sourdough bread and have made delicious pastries with an all-natural healthy approach since 2015. We were pioneers of sourdough long-fermented bread in Ukraine, and in October 2021 we finally opened the very new bakery – Bakehouse Garage – in the Podil district of Kyiv. This is the bakery of my dreams, and we spent three years and 1.5 million US dollars on building this bakery. But during the first days of the war, we had attacks and explosions just a few kilometres from it, so we had to close it on 24 February. Instead we baked in the basement of the old bakery.

From day three of the war, my team have baked bread and given it for free to our soldiers, hospitals, people in cities and villages hurt by the Russians, and the elderly of Kyiv. Our bakers make 450–1,000 charity loaves every day. And we will continue to bake them as long as our country needs them.

It is challenging – to bake in a warzone. It is hard to find and deliver good ingredients, and the logistics of team members has been challenging, as not all the members of our team are able to come and work. And women face a different challenge: many of us, especially those who have small children, left Kyiv and moved to Western Ukraine or abroad so we did not have to hear the sirens or go to bomb shelters with babies and toddlers tens of times a day. So many chefs, bakers and office staff (primarily women) left the country. And no one knows when we will come back.

I believe no citizen of the world should stay silent and indifferent to the terror of war. And my gratitude to all the bakers who invested their time and attention in creating this book knows no bounds. We, bakers, create. And this is the opposite of what fascist aggressors do every day. We need peace, so let's knead it, helping Ukrainians fight for victory and survive this horror.

—Anna Makievska
The Bakehouse, Kyiv

Sixty-five bakers from around the world donated the recipes in this book to raise money for Ukraine. Here are some of their faces. Top to bottom, left to right: Fortitude Bakehouse, Yotam Ottolenghi, Cindy Zurias, Beesham Soogrim, Kitty Tait, Helen Goh, Max Blachman-Gentile, Michael James, Lance Gardner and Angharad Conway, SCHOON, Matthew Jones, Sally Clarke, Sarah Johnson, Wayne Caddy.

Being a baker is to experience humanity on its most fundamental and humbling levels, providing both the most basic daily bread and the soft, intricate sticky treats that light up a child's face. I don't think I've ever felt this more than I have after the honour of speaking with Anna who runs The Bakehouse in Kyiv. She is truly inspirational!

Throughout the horrors and turmoil of the war, Anna and her team have continued to bake day and night in order to feed the people of Ukraine. It is impossible to express how humbling their effort is in the face of such hardship; the power, generosity and defiance that they show is truly awe inspiring.

Knead Peace was born from the idea that baking is a community that has the power to make a difference from the war, hatred, violence and knife and gun crimes that have caused so much pain in today's world. *Knead Peace* the cookbook marks the first of many projects being planned.

It has been truly amazing to see the generosity and humanity of the baking and creative community who took on the task of making the *Knead Peace* cookbook. I must firstly thank Anna and her staff at The Bakehouse in Ukraine for her time and generosity through these horrendous times. To all the bakers and chefs that have generously donated their recipes and time, who have made this into it the book it is, I am eternally grateful for your contributions. The *Knead Peace* cookbook truly owes a massive thank you to Jessica Wang, Rollo Scott, Judith Hannam, Kate Thomas, Sarah and Haydn Thomas, Michael Green, Jessica Gully, Grace Percival and my wife Marilize Green for their dedication and hard work in making this happen.

—Andrew Green
Knead Peace

BREAD

Ben MacKinnon
E5 BAKEHOUSE

Makes
200g leaven

Sourdough Starter & Leaven

A starter is a renewable sample of naturally fermenting flour and water, which can be used as the first building block in the process of making any sourdough bread. Starters can be built into leavens, which can be built into doughs, which are then shaped and finally baked into breads.

INGREDIENTS

RYE SOURDOUGH STARTER

I litre	water, at room temperature
330g	organic stoneground wholemeal rye flour

RYE SOURDOUGH LEAVEN

20g	Rye Sourdough Starter (see above)
120g	water
60g	wholemeal rye flour

STARTER METHOD

DAY I

1. In the evening, fill your jug with I litre of water from the cold tap and leave it to stand at room temperature. This will allow any chlorine (which might be harmful to the yeasts and bacteria you are going to try to cultivate) to evaporate before you use it.

DAY 2

2. In the evening, pour 60ml of the jug water into a large plastic container. Add 30g wholemeal rye flour. Mix them together with a fork until the flour is completely hydrated. Secure the lid with clips and leave at room temperature for 12 hours.

DAYS 3–12

3. In the morning refill the jug with tap water.

4. In the evening, pour all of your mixture into a clean cup or bowl. Rinse your plastic container and lid with water.

5. Now weigh 10g of your culture back into your plastic container. Add 60ml of the jug water, 30g wholemeal rye flour and mix

them all together with a fork. Leave at room temperature for another 12 hours.

6. Repeat steps 3–5 every day – preferably at the same time each day for 10 days.

7. On the last evening of your 10 days, refresh your starter as usual. In the morning, when you find it nice and bubbly, put it in the fridge. This will slow the fermentation right down so that from now on, rather than feeding your starter every day, you can feed it once a week.

8. In the future, whenever you want to make a loaf of bread (for any of the recipes in the book), you are going to take a small quantity of starter from your pot and then use it as the first building block in the process.

LEAVEN METHOD

DAY 1

1. Take your starter out of the fridge and weigh 20g into a small mixing bowl. Add the 120g water and mix them together. Then add the 60g wholemeal rye flour and mix again.

2. Cover the bowl with a tea towel and leave it out overnight (don't forget to put your starter back in the fridge).

DAY 2

3. In the morning, take a little teaspoon of the mixture and drop it into a glass of water, where it should float. You now have about 200g of rye leaven.

SOURDOUGH TERMINOLOGY

ACTIVE
Your starter is activated through the refreshing process, making it vibrant and bubbly. The refreshing process is described in steps 3–5 of the Starter Method. This can also be called feeding the starter.

RIPE
Your starter is ripe once it has doubled in size after its feeding. This will take approx. 8 hours. It is now ready to be used in baking.

HYDRATION
This is the ratio of water to flour in a sourdough starter. The hydration is calculated by dividing the total amount of water by the total amount of flour. Refreshing your starter with equal amounts of flour and water will result in 100% hydration.

STIFF vs LIQUID
A stiff sourdough starter has a hydration of 50%, i.e. you have used half as much water as flour in the refreshment. A liquid starter has a hydration of 500%, i.e. you have used 5 times as much water as flour in the refreshment.

Simple Sourdough

INGREDIENTS

400g	strong white bread flour
100g	strong wholemeal flour
320g	water
120g	active Sourdough Starter (fed the night before) (see pages 12–13)
15g	salt

METHOD

DAY 1

1. Mix the flours and water until well incorporated. Then cover and let it sit at room temperature for 1 hour. After the hour, add the sourdough starter and salt. Mix by hand until well incorporated.

2. Place the dough on a work surface – without flour. Do 5 minutes of slap and fold technique (see opposite) to knead the dough. Place the dough in a container and let it relax for 30 minutes.

3. Do 3 sets of stretch and fold (see page 26, step 8) at 30-minute intervals and after the final one, end with a 30-minute rest.

4. Place the dough in a container 3 times larger than the dough, and cover with a tea towel. Place in the refrigerator overnight to ferment.

DAY 2

5. Divide and shape: place the dough on a lightly floured work surface and flour the dough scraper to divide the dough into 2 pieces. Pre-shape the dough, cover and then leave to rest for 30 minutes.

6. Once rested, shape the dough into round loaves and place in a floured proving basket seam-side up. Once shaped, cover with clingfilm (plastic wrap) and let them prove for 2 hours in a warm area.

7. Preheat the oven for 1 hour at 250°C (500°F), Gas Mark 10, with a Dutch oven (casserole dish) inside.

8. Score each loaf just before going in the oven.

9. Gently tip a loaf on to a sheet of nonstick baking paper and gently place inside the Dutch oven. Spray the loaf with a fine mist of water and place the lid on top.

10. Bake with steam for 10 minutes. Lower the temperature to 210°C (410°F), Gas Mark 6 and bake for an additional 25 minutes or so with the lid off. Repeat with the second loaf.

TIP: To knead using the slap and fold technique, lift your dough off the work surface, holding it out in front of you. Slap the dough back down onto the work surface, so that the lower half lands on the surface, and you are holding up the top half. Then fold the top half over the lower half, trapping air inside the dough. Repeat the process until the dough becomes smooth.

Seeds for Solidarity Porridge

My team and I felt a wave of rage, frustration and helplessness as we watched events unfold since the war began. I have learned that emotions, when used as currency, can be used to fuel action. This recipe has been created by a whole team of people, including Team Hart bakery, Max at Sourdough Revolution and Dan, my business partner. The porridge can be used in any standard sourdough recipe. We have carefully tailored it to ensure it can easily be integrated into breads in a professional bakery while still being suitable for domestic baking. It also happens to be delicious, with a natural, malted, treacly sweetness.

INGREDIENTS

20g	sprouted barley (this takes 2 days)
30g	wholemeal rye flour
20g	poppy seeds
20g	sunflower seeds
10g	lightly toasted coriander seeds
approx. 240g water	

METHOD

1. Sprout the barley in advance; it will take around two days. Note that only whole grains, not polished ones, will sprout. Rinse the grains in water, and then leave them to soak overnight in water. Drain, rinse then drain again. Place in a jar with holes in the lid, or wrap in fine cotton or muslin and secure with an elastic band. Leave to sprout, rinsing every day. Once tiny shoots appear on the grains the barley is ready to use.

2. Combine the flour, seeds and sprouted barley in a saucepan. Add 120g of the water and put the pan over a low heat.

3. Stir, making sure the mixture doesn't catch on the bottom of the pan. As the porridge thickens, gradually add the remaining water and keep stirring.

4. Continue simmering and stirring until the porridge has reached the right consistency

(continued)

(see my tip below). It's important that you don't add too much water, but equally important that the porridge isn't under-hydrated. It's difficult to give you a precise measurement for how much water you will need to get this balance right, because every grain and seed in the porridge mix will hydrate slightly differently. What you have to do is ensure the porridge is thoroughly cooked, which can take a good 8–10 minutes of standing over the pan and stirring.

TIP: Remember that in order for the porridge to add to the gelatinization of a sourdough bread, the ingredients have to be fully hydrated. My tip is that it is always good for the mixture to end up looking slightly more liquid than you think it should be, because it will continue to take up water and thicken when you take the pan off the heat and leave the porridge to cool.

TIP: You can use this method in any existing standard sourdough recipes, for example the Simple Sourdough on pages 14–15. After the dough has been mixed and the gluten has developed, weigh your dough, then add 10% of that weight in porridge to the bowl. Mix, prove, shape and bake as usual.

Anna Makievska
THE BAKEHOUSE

Makes
4 LOAVES

Flaxseed Sourdough

Flaxseed bread, or The Flax, as we started to call it as soon as it became popular among our customers, was the first bread we baked with my recipe on a commercial scale. Flax is rich in fibre, loaded with omega-3 fatty acids and has a lot more benefits for our health. And it can be locally sourced. So, to the point: here is the recipe for our most popular bread.

INGREDIENTS

SOAKED FLAXSEEDS

260g	flaxseeds
260g	water, at room-temperature

LIQUID LEAVEN

155g	strong white bread flour
155g	water
35g	Sourdough Starter (pages 12–13) (100% hydration)

SOURDOUGH

430g	strong white bread flour
430g	strong wholemeal flour
650g	water
28g	sea salt flakes

METHOD

1. Soak the flaxseed 12–24 hours before mixing the dough: mix the flaxseed with the room-temperature water in a container. Cover it with a lid and leave it on the counter.

2. Make the liquid leaven approx. 7–8 hours before mixing the dough: it's best to do it overnight or first thing in the morning, so you can start mixing the dough in the afternoon. Mix together the bread flour, water and liquid, ripe sourdough starter, cover with a tea towel and then leave it for 7–8 hours.

3. When the leaven is bubbly, smells like yogurt and has grown in volume 2.5–3 times, it's good to go in the dough!

4. For the dough, mix the white bread flour, wholemeal flour, water and the leaven in a bowl. If mixing by hand, mix until homogeneous and smooth; if using a stand mixer, mix on speed 1 until smooth.

5. Cover with a tea towel and leave for 40 minutes to 1½ hours to rest.

(continued)

6. Then add the salt and the soaked flaxseeds and mix thoroughly using your hands or on speed 1 in the mixer. The dough will be quite wet and soft and will need to be mixed for a while to pass the windowpane test.

7. After mixing, the dough's temperature should be around 23–25°C (73–77°F). Now your dough should rest at room temperature for 2½–4 hours, depending on your climate conditions and the initial temperature of the dough. During this time, you need to stretch and fold the dough (see page 26, step 9) approx. every 45 minutes.

8. Divide into 600g pieces of dough; the batch should be just enough for 4 loaves. Round the dough, place on a tray and cover for 40 minutes.

9. Shape the dough into either a boule or batard shape (round or oval) using common bread shaping techniques (see page 26, step 9) and then put in the thoroughly floured proofing baskets, seam-side up.

10. Now you can put your loaves into the refrigerator for at least 12 hours (I recommend up to 48 hours).

11. Take the loaves out of the refrigerator about 30–60 minutes before you are ready to bake.

12. Preheat the oven for 1 hour at 250°C (500°F), Gas Mark 10, with a Dutch oven (casserole dish) inside.

13. Lightly flour several sheets of baking paper, then gently tip the loaves out of the proofing baskets on to the paper. Score with a very sharp knife. Carefully lower one loaf with the paper into the Dutch oven. Spray with water and place into the oven with the lid on.

14. Bake for 15 minutes with the lid and then lower the temperature to 230°C (450°F), Gas Mark 8, and bake for 15 more minutes without the lid. Repeat with the following 3 loaves.

15. When cooked, the bread will sound hollow when tapped on the bottom. Leave to cool on a wire rack once baked.

TIP: To check the dough using the windowpane test, take a small ball of dough and stretch it so that the dough is thin enough for light to pass through. If it can't be stretched thin enough without tearing then it is not yet ready, and should be kneaded further.

Challah Buns

INGREDIENTS

1	egg
1	egg yolk

pinch of salt
vegetable oil, for greasing
sesame seeds (optional)

FIRM LEAVEN

110g	T65 (French white bread) flour
65g	water
6g	wheat starter

CHALLAH DOUGH

550g	T65 (French white bread) flour
12g	salt
3g	instant dried yeast
100g	egg yolk
65g	honey
210ml	water
180ml	mature Firm Leaven (see above)

METHOD

1. For the eggwash, whisk together the whole egg and egg yolk in a bowl, and then add a pinch of salt. Pass the mixture through a sieve into a small bowl and store, covered, in the refrigerator overnight.

2. For the firm leaven, mix the flour, water and starter together in a bowl and cover with a tea towel. Allow to ferment for 12–18 hours at room temperature. The leaven is then ready to add to the dough.

3. For the dough, add all of the ingredients to the mixing bowl of a stand mixer fitted with a dough hook, and proceed to mix on a slow speed until thoroughly combined.

4. Move to a faster speed until the soft dough totally picks up and clears the mixing bowl and is wrapped fully around the dough hook. The dough should look soft and silky.

5. Place the dough in a lightly oiled bowl and cover with clingfilm (plastic wrap). Allow the dough to rest for 30 minutes and then apply a fold or knock back.

6. Cover again and place in the refrigerator overnight for a minimum of 12 hours, to a maximum of 48 hours.

7. After the 12 hours, tip out the dough on to a work surface and, using a dough scraper, portion into 120g pieces or 10 equal portions, and round into smooth balls.

8. Line 2 baking trays (sheets) with nonstick baking paper. Place 5 balls per tray in a 2, 1, 2 formation and evenly apply the eggwash with a pastry brush. Prove in the oven with a tub of very hot water at the base for up to 2 hours or until double in size; a good test is to jiggle the tray and if there is a wobble to the bun, then it is ready to bake. If there is no wobble, allow further proving time. You may need to refresh the water every 30–45 minutes.

9. Remove from the makeshift oven-prover and turn on the oven to 230°C (450°F), Gas Mark 8.

10. While the oven is heating up, apply a second coat of eggwash. If you wish to use sesame seeds, then this is the time to apply a sprinkle. When the oven is up to the correct temperature, place the challah buns into the oven and bake until golden brown or for approx. 13 minutes. Remove and allow to cool.

Rye & Fennel Sourdough

INGREDIENTS

RYE LEAVEN

20ml	water
170g	wholemeal rye flour
220g	Rye Sourdough Starter (see pages 12–13)

MAIN DOUGH

345g	Rye Leaven (see above)
205ml	water
125g	wholemeal rye flour, plus extra for dusting
125g	strong white bread flour
10g	fennel seeds
9g	fine sea salt

METHOD

1. The night before you are going to make your bread, you need to prepare your leaven. You are going to need 410g for the final dough so you might as well round it up to easy numbers (and give yourself a bit extra to play with).

2. Mix the leaven ingredients together, cover with a tea towel and leave out overnight (don't forget to put your starter pot back in the refrigerator).

3. In the morning, it should be nice and bubbly with a pleasant balance of sweetness and acidity. Drop a teaspoon of the mixture in a glass of water. Does it float? If so it's ready to use. If you make 410g, this will leave approx. 65g as starter for future baking starter leaven.

4. For the dough, place the wet ingredients in one bowl and the dry, except the salt, in another.

5. Mix the water and the leaven together until well combined.

6. Add the dry ingredients and, with your hands, mix everything together, making sure to fully hydrate the flour and that there are no dry pieces in the dough. Cover and leave for 20 minutes.

(continued)

7. Mix in the salt with your hands, then cover and let it rest for 30 minutes.

8. Stretch and fold the dough, pulling up one edge and folding into the centre (like you're trying to make it into an envelope). Rotate the dough 90 degrees and repeat, stretching and folding into the centre a total of 4 times. It will help if you wet your fingertips with a little water before doing this. Don't worry if you have to skip a fold. Double it next time around. Repeat this entire process a further 3 times, at 30 minute intervals. The folding is to stretch and align the gluten bonds that are forming, so that you end up with a nice elastic/extensible dough.

9. Once the final fold and stretch and fold has been completed, it's time to shape the dough into a ball. Fold all the edges of the dough in and then with cupped hands shape into a ball using your hands in a circular motion. Then dip the loaf seam-side down into some rye flour and place that side into a floured proving basket.

10. Leave to prove in a warm place for 1–1½ hours.

11. Preheat the oven to its highest temperature with an empty Dutch oven (casserole dish) inside.

12. Take the preheated Dutch oven out of the oven, being very careful not to burn yourself. Scatter a piece of nonstick baking paper with semolina (the semolina will stop the dough from sticking), then tip your loaf out of the proving basket on to the baking paper.

13. Carefully lower the loaf with the paper into the casserole dish. Gently spray the loaf with a fine mist of water, place the lid on and place in the oven.

14. Bake for 25 minutes with the lid on. Remove the lid and bake for a further 10 minutes. Keep an eye on it but try not to open the door too much. Take it out when it looks nicely burnished.

TIP: The Dutch oven with lid creates the closest equivalent of baking with steam (the bread creates its own moisture/steam which surrounds the bread and prevents it from forming a crust too soon).

Kate Marton
HYLSTEN BAKERY

Makes
2 LOAVES

Townmill Tin Loaf

INGREDIENTS

see note at end of recipe about flour types

605g	Ölands flour (stoneground white flour)
365g	Miller's Choice flour (stoneground white flour)
245g	Red Lammas flour (stoneground white flour)
850g	water, plus 60g, for bassinage
245g	stiff Wholemeal Leaven (see pages 12–13, use wholemeal flour in place of Rye)
30g	salt
oil, for greasing	

METHOD

1. First place all the flours in a large mixing bowl. When preparing to mix the dough, be aware that you are aiming for a dough temperature of 28°C (82.5°F); the temperature of the water is the main tool you have for controlling this, so choose your water temperature accordingly.

2. As you are hand-mixing this, it is okay to mix everything together at once. However, if the water temperature you have chosen is over 40°C (104°F), then be careful to mix the flour and water together a little first before introducing the leaven so as not to scald it.

3. Mix thoroughly until you can no longer see any dry flour. This should take at least a few minutes. Cover the dough and leave it to rest for 30 minutes.

4. Once rested, check the dough for its hydration. If you think it could take some more water, you can add the bassinage. Use your fingers to squeeze the water through the dough, folding as you go.

5. Once the water is fully distributed, fold the dough to neaten it up. Rest for another 30 minutes and then fold the dough again. Repeat this another 2 or 3 times, keeping an eye on the fermentation. If the dough is moving quickly, you could leave out the last fold.

(continued)

6. The bulk fermentation is usually around 2½–3 hours long but this can vary depending on the dough temperature and the ambient temperature of the room.

7. Once you are happy with the bulk fermentation, prepare your tins by brushing them with a small amount of oil.

8. Tip the dough on to a work surface and scale it to 2 x 1200g pieces. Round these slightly to create some tension before placing them gently into the tins. We use 2700ml capacity tins but you could split this into a few more smaller loaves if you'd like.

9. As the bread proves and approaches the top of the tin, preheat the oven to 250°C (500°F), Gas Mark 10.

10. Once the dough has reached the top of the tin, place it in the oven, preferably on a baking stone with a tray of boiling water underneath to create some steam in the oven.

11. Drop the oven temperature down to 220°C (425°F), Gas Mark 7, and bake for 40 minutes or until the loaf is fully baked and the crust is your desired colour.

12. You can remove the tin for the last 5–10 minutes of baking. Note: we don't score our tin loaves and we are looking to maximize the proving of the dough as it has the support of the tin to max out its potential. This should result in a beautiful honeycomb crumb.

NOTES

This recipe is the exact recipe we use at the bakery for our Tin Loaf. We use freshly milled stoneground flour from our miller Andrew at Fresh Flour Company. You can use a variety of flours in this recipe. The variety of grain we have access to changes regularly and this is our base recipe. The hydration is the main thing that varies when we change the flour so be mindful of this when testing out different flours. We would encourage you to use high extraction stoneground flours as these are much more nutritious and delicious than standard roller mill flour that is more readily available in the shops. You can buy retail bags of stoneground flour from Gilchesters, which specializes in heritage varieties of grain. We use a stiff and mature wholemeal leaven, but you can experiment with your own leaven here.

English Muffins

INGREDIENTS

300g	plain (all-purpose) flour, plus extra for dusting
245g	strong white bread flour
8g	fast-action (active) dried yeast
14g	fine table salt
16g	caster (superfine) sugar
55g	unsalted butter, softened
1	egg
180g	full-fat (whole) milk
180g	warm water

oil, for greasing
semolina, for dusting

METHOD

1. Place the flours in a large mixing bowl. Sprinkle the dried yeast on one side of the flour and the salt on the other side.

2. Add the sugar, butter, egg and milk, then mix all the ingredients together to make a soft dough. Using a stand mixer with a dough hook, mix for 10 minutes until the dough is soft and stretchy.

3. Place the dough in a large, oiled bowl, cover and leave to rise until doubled in size.

4. Dust a work surface lightly with flour. Place the dough on the floured surface and weigh it out into 80g pieces.

5. Lightly dust 2 baking trays (sheets) with semolina. Shape each piece of dough into a ball. Place 6 greased metal rings on each tray and place a piece of dough into each ring.

6. Cover the muffins and leave to prove until doubled in size.

7. Preheat the oven to 170°C (335°F), Gas Mark 3.

8. Bake the muffins in the oven for 20 minutes. Then carefully turn each muffin ring over and cook for a further 5 minutes.

Beetroot & Rye Sourdough

INGREDIENTS

250g	beetroots (beets)
400g	strong white bread flour, plus extra for dusting
75g	wholemeal flour
25g	rye flour
275g	water
125g	mature Rye Sourdough Leaven (see pages 12–13)
11g	salt

METHOD

BEETROOTS (BEETS)

1. Preheat the oven to 200°C (400°F), Gas Mark 6.

2. Wash the beetroots and place them on a baking tray (sheet).

3. Roast in the oven for 45 minutes or so – until they feel soft when inserting a fork.

4. Let them cool and then rub the skin off before puréeing in a blender. Do not worry about some remaining small solid pieces.

DOUGH

DAY 1

1. Mix the beetroot (beet) purée with the flours and water until well incorporated. Cover and let it sit at room temperature for 1 hour.

2. After the hour, add the leaven and salt. Mix by hand until well incorporated. Place the dough on a work surface – without flour.

3. Do 5 minutes of slap and fold technique to knead the dough (see page 15). Place the

(continued)

dough in a container, cover with a teal towel and let it relax for 30 minutes.

4. Do 3 sets of stretch and fold (see page 26, step 8) at 30-minute intervals, and after the final one, end with a 30-minute rest.

DAY 2

5. Cover the dough and place in the refrigerator overnight to ferment in a container 3 times larger than the dough.

6. Place the dough on a lightly floured work surface and flour the dough scraper to divide dough into 2 pieces of approx. 550g.

7. There is no need to do a pre-shape with this dough, so you can shape into a round loaf straight away and place in a floured proving basket with the seam side on the top. Once shaped, cover with clingfilm (plastic wrap) and let it prove for about 2 hours in a warm area.

8. Preheat the oven for 1 hour at 250°C (500°F), Gas Mark 10, with a shallow roasting pan on the bottom shelf of the oven. Line a baking tray (sheet) with nonstick baking paper.

9. Gently tip the loaf on to the lined tray. Score the loaf with a simple cut lengthways just before going in the oven.

10. Place the loaf in the oven, add boiling water to the roasting pan at the bottom of the oven and quickly close the door. Bake with steam for 10 minutes.

11. Lower the temperature to 210°C (410°F), Gas Mark 6, and remove the roasting pan of water. Bake for an additional 25 minutes.

Makes
1 LOAF

White Potato Sourdough

We use a stiff starter in our sourdoughs; this is for several reasons – we now use about 100kg starter a day and find it easier to control with less hydration; it has a lovely flavour profile, not too acidic; and more than anything, it cleans the mixer at the end of our shift. Assuming you already have a starter ready to use, just feed it with 60% hydration and ensure that it is lively and ripe when you start to make this bread.

INGREDIENTS

460g	strong white bread flour
275ml	warm water, at around 27°C (80.5°F)
120g	active, stiff Sourdough Starter (see pages 12–13)
50ml	water
15g	salt
70g	white potato

METHOD

1. Use warm water – 27°C (80.5°F) may seem high, but small amounts of dough get cold quickly, so you need a bit of warmth to get everything going. With your hands or in a stand mixer with a dough hook, mix the flour and add the 275ml water until you have no dry bits and no wet bits. Cover with a tea towel and leave for at least 45 minutes, but no longer than 1 hour.

2. Now add your starter to the first mix, squashing it in with your fingers, followed by the 50ml water and salt. This will break the dough up, go slimy and feel wrong. But don't worry, it'll come back together if you just keep mixing it.

3. Once you have a dough that is coherent (about 8 minutes by hand), scrape your bowl down and cover it for 45 minutes.

4. Grate the potato on the coarse setting of a box grater, skin and all, and rinse under very hot water to remove the starch. Once rinsed, use your hands to squeeze out as much water as you can from the grated potato.

(continued)

5. Tip the potato on to the dough and using wet hands, grab an edge of the dough and fold it over the top of the potato. Turn your bowl 90 degrees and repeat. Do this 4 times in total (north, south, east and west if the bowl was the world). Scrape your bowl and rest it somewhere nice and warm for 1 hour.

6. Repeat this 3 times until you have given your dough 4 folds in total.

7. Now leave your dough to ferment until it is puffy and like a wobbly belly, full of life and bubbles but not feeling like it will deflate if you prod it. The time this takes will vary on the temperature of your kitchen and a million other variables, but go with your instinct and practice – you will soon get the sweet spot. It's likely to take a further 30 minutes but may take up to 2 hours. We like to push our dough far at this stage, so sit back and let the magic happen!

8. Shaping your loaf is tricky and takes practise, so be kind to yourself, working confidently; as with most things, the more you practice the easier it gets. You want to work with as little flour as possible. Carefully turn your dough out on to a work surface, grab one edge, stretch it to the air and fold it over the dough to the other side, working your way around the dough, folding the edges in until you have a wonton-style round. Flip this and rest it. You want this to be tight and as circular as possible. Pop this into a banneton (proving basket), seam-side up (smooth-side down). If you don't have a banneton, flour the hell out of a tea towel, line a bowl with it and use this.

9. Chuck it in the refrigerator for at least 6 hours, but up to 24 hours.

10. Preheat the oven to 250°C (500°F), Gas Mark 10, with a Dutch oven (casserole dish) inside.

11. Turn your dough out on to a piece of nonstick baking paper, confidently slash the top once, holding your sharpest knife at an angle as parallel to the dough as possible. Use the baking paper as a little hammock to lower the loaf into the dish (no dish? Don't panic – a baking tray/sheet will be fine). Pour half a cup of water into the bottom of the dish, ideally under the baking paper, put the lid on, and put it straight into the oven. Reduce the temperature to 225°C (435°F), Gas Mark 7, and bake for 30 minutes.

12. Take the lid off and bake for a further 15 minutes (or until you have a lovely dark deep coloured crust – be bold with your bake). Let the loaf cool before you cut into it, however tempting it might be!

Pretzels

INGREDIENTS

DOUGH

250g	mature sourdough starter (see page 12)
850g	strong white bread flour, plus extra for dusting
408ml	water, at around 35°C/95°F (to achieve the right desired dough temperature)
17g	fine sea salt
60g	unsalted butter
3g	diastatic malt powder

LYE BATH

500ml–1 litre water
30g   lye pearls
OR
3 tbsp   bicarbonate of soda (baking soda)
coarse sea salt granules, for sprinkling

METHOD

1. Feed your mature starter at 9pm the evening before with a 1:10:10 ratio. Store in a clean jar and keep at around 24°C (75°F). It should double/triple in size within 10–12 hours. Let it ferment until it nearly peaks, then just before peak (the next morning), it is ready to be used.

2. The next day at around 8am it is time to make your dough.

3. For this dough you need to aim for a dough temperature of around 24°C (75°F). If you have a particularly hot or cold environment, you may want to use much colder or much hotter water to achieve the desired temperature.

4. Combine the flour, water, salt, softened butter, malt powder and mature leaven in a bowl and mix together with your hands. If using a mixer, do this on Speed 2 for a couple of minutes.

5. Note on mechanical kneading: if you are using a mixer fitted with a spiral dough hook, make sure to really watch the machine. It is an incredibly stiff dough so you may cause damage to your machine. You can start off in the machine and finish off by hand. You are the best judge of your equipment.

(continued)

6. Now it is time to develop gluten by kneading. This can be done mechanically or by hand. If you do it mechanically, mix on speed 3 for 3–5 minutes. By hand use the slap and fold method (see page 15) or by using the same movement you would for making pasta dough: stretch out with one hand and scrape back together by folding over on the work surface until you can see the dough coming together and the gluten no longer ripping.

7. Place the dough in a bowl and cover with clingfilm (plastic wrap). Check the dough temperature at this stage and set a timer for the bulk fermentation time according to the temperature: if the dough is 24°C (75°F), it should take about 3 hours.

8. Very lightly dust a work surface with flour and tip out the dough. Divide it up into 115g pieces using scales and a dough scraper to cut the dough. Then, using your hands, heavily de-gas, or knock back, each piece, then shape roughly into a rectangle. Slightly flatten and fold a small part of the dough down and press the seam in, then repeat with the next bit. Keep on folding the dough over the next piece until you arrive at the other end. Repeat with the other pieces until you have 13 cigars. Cover with a tea towel or a plastic bag and leave to rest for 15 minutes.

9. Final shape at 12:45pm: line 2 large baking trays (sheets) with nonstick baking paper and set them aside. Starting with a pre-shaped piece of dough, place it in front of you and place your hands on top, leaving a 3cm (1¼-inch) gap right in the middle between your thumbs. Roll out wide and long with a strong, firm stretching movement that creates evenness and a 60cm (24-inch)-long sausage. The centre should remain thick and untouched. If you feel resistance and elasticity, leave it for a minute and then continue; it might just need to relax a bit.

10. Pull both ends up so that you arrange a big loop with the base of the loop being the thick middle, fold over the loops twice in a twist and then arrange each on one side of the loop so you create a pretzel shape. Press down to seal. Then transfer the shaped pretzels on to the prepared baking tray. Repeat until all pretzels have been pre-shaped. You don't need to leave a large gap between the pretzels, as you will pick them up once again. Cover them with a large plastic bag or turkey roasting bag.

11. Final prove at 1:00pm: leave the pretzels to prove for 30 minutes, covered, at room temperature and then 1 hour in the refrigerator, uncovered. It is important to chill the pretzels properly and let a skin form. You can at this stage also place them in the refrigerator overnight ready for the next day.

12. Lye bath at 2:30pm: preheat the oven to 250°C (500°F), Gas Mark 10 and set up a lye station. At this point you can decide whether you want to use lye (see Steps 12–13) or choose bicarbonate of soda (baking soda) instead (see Step 14).

13. For the lye bath, prepare a large bowl or glass dish with 500ml water and a 3% lye solution. If you have lye pearls it would be 15g lye pearls, for example. Wear gloves at all times and carefully place this mixture on a baking tray (sheet) lined with nonstick baking paper. Next to it, place another baking tray lined with baking paper and if there is any gap between them, line that with baking paper too. You don't want any lye on the surface as it will corrode. Your ultimate goal is to have a production line where you take your pretzel from the baking tray, dip in lye and place on the new baking tray. Then score and bake.

14. Once the station is set up, wearing gloves, place a pretzel in the lye solution, leave for a second and transfer to the new baking

tray. Repeat with all pretzels, then score the pretzels, still using gloves, and set them aside. Clean up your station first to avoid any accidents and wash your hands. Then, sprinkle coarse sea salt granules over the pretzels and bake them immediately.

15. Alternatively, you can set up a station with a large saucepan and add 1 litre of water and 3 tablespoons of bicarbonate of soda (baking soda). Bring to the boil, then place 1 pretzel at a time for 40 seconds in the boiling water. Remove with a slotted spoon and place back on to the baking tray. Then repeat with the remaining pretzels. Be careful, as they may start falling apart while lifting out of the water, so just arrange them again quickly. Score them, sprinkle over sea salt granules and bake immediately.

16. Bake at 3:00pm: place the baking trays in the oven and bake for 10 minutes, then lower the heat to 220°C (425°F), Gas Mark 7, and bake for a further 8–10 minutes until they are golden and shiny.

17. Remove and leave to cool on a wire rack.

Lazy Wholemeal Loaf

This method is much like that of focaccia – the folding part is essential for really developing the gluten. The key is to keep the dough warm throughout the whole process, as this will create a really flavourful and well-developed loaf. I like this approach to baking as it is very gentle and stress free. It may come across as quite unorthodox, but trust me, it really works. From time to time we can all break the rules, as long as it tastes great.

INGREDIENTS

150g	Sourdough Starter (made with white flour, see pages 12–13)
350g	warm water
400g	strong wholemeal flour
8g	fine sea salt

oil, for greasing

METHOD

1. Put the starter and warm water into a mixing bowl and break up the starter in the water with your hands. Add the flour and salt and bring together into a rough dough, then tip it out on to a work surface and knead for about 5 minutes until you have a smooth, elasticated dough.

2. Lightly oil a mixing bowl and return the dough to the bowl. Cover with a shower cap or a damp tea towel and leave at room temperature, ideally somewhere warm, for I hour.

3. Give the dough a fold, cover and leave to rest for a further I hour. Give the dough a second fold, cover and leave to rest for another I hour. Give the dough a third and final fold and rest for a final I hour. After the final hour of proving, the dough should have a total of 3 folds and 4 hours of resting time.

4. Preheat the oven to 230°C (450°F), Gas Mark 8. If baking your loaf in a Dutch oven (casserole dish), place it in the oven to warm up. Alternatively, you can lightly oil a 900g (2lb) loaf tin.

5. Remove the dough from the bowl and shape it according to how you will bake it. Form it into a round if baking in a Dutch oven, (casserole dish) or into a standard loaf shape if baking in a tin.

6. To bake in a Dutch oven, carefully remove the dish from the oven and gently place the dough inside. Cover with the lid and bake for 30 minutes. Remove the lid and bake for a further 10 minutes.

7. To bake in a tin, place the tin on the middle shelf of the oven and put a tray filled with $\frac{1}{4}$ cup of water on the bottom of the oven to create steam. Bake for 30 minutes, then turn the tin around and bake for a final 10 minutes.

8. Remove the baked loaf from the oven and leave to cool completely before slicing.

Anca Tînc
ILLE BRØD

Makes
1 LOAF

Swidden Rye Sourdough

Swidden rye was brought to Norway in the 60s and it's been a bakers' favourite thanks to its sweet flavour. It is one of my go-tos when it comes to baking at home, since I like to mill it on spot, both coarse and fine, to play a bit with the final texture. I often mix it with another wholegrain, be it barley (and add some nuts and dried fruit) or einkorn. Baked in a tin, it becomes a very easy-to-make bread.

INGREDIENTS

100g	swidden rye berries, for sprouting
100g	young Rye Leaven (see page 45)
450g	lukewarm water, plus extra if needed
100g	wholemeal coarse swidden rye
300g	wholemeal fine swidden rye
100g	wholemeal fine einkorn (or any other wholemeal you have at hand)
13g	sea salt flakes
200g	sunflower seeds, for coating

METHOD

1. Two days before making the bread, rinse the rye berries in water and let them soak for 24 hours at room temperature.

2. The next day, rinse and drain them well. Put them in a jar with a loose cover/cheesecloth and let them sprout, giving them a shake every now and then, making sure they're still moist. Sprinkle with some water if they are drying out. Once they sprout, they're ready to go.

3. Prepare a rye leaven (equal quantities of water, rye flour and starter). Keep it in a warm place for 3–4 hours and do the floating test (see page 24, Step 3) before using it. The leaven should be bubbly and smell like yogurt.

4. Once the leaven is ready, mix the lukewarm water, leaven and flours in a bowl. Cover it and let it rest for 30–40 minutes in a warm place. If your kitchen is very cold, you can keep the bowl in the oven, with the light on.

5. Add the salt and the sprouted rye to the dough. If the dough is dry, add another 10–15g

(continued)

of water. Let the dough sit in a warm place for another 3–3½ hours and check it from time to time, to see how the smell changes (from grassy and sweet to slightly fruity and sour). You'll also notice an increase in volume.

6. Put the sunflower seeds in a shallow tray. Oil a 26 × 11 × 6cm (10½ × 4½ × 2½-inch) metal loaf tin (pan).

7. When the time is up, flip the dough on to a work surface and, with wet hands, shape it into an oval. Use a scraper to lift it and drop it in the tray with the sunflower seeds. Coat the dough with seeds and put it in the tin. Put the bread in the refrigerator overnight (for at least 16 hours).

8. The next day, preheat the oven to 230°C (450°F), Gas Mark 8.

9. Take the tin out of the refrigerator and spray the top of the dough with water. Put it in the oven, drop the temperature to 210°C (410°F), Gas Mark 6, and bake it for 25 minutes.

10. Reduce the temperature to 180°C (350°C), Gas Mark 4, and then bake it for another 35–40 minutes. Check the inside temperature of the bread with a probe and make sure it's over 97°C (207°F).

11. Flip the tin on a cooling rack and let the bread cool down. Make sure to rest it for another 3–4 hours before cutting it. Enjoy!

Richard Hart
HART BAGERI

Makes
I LOAF

Danish Deluxe Super Seeded Rye

The deluxe super seeded rye is a spin on the super seeded rye that we sell at the bakery. The classic loaf already has more seeds than flour by weight, and this version uses even more varieties of seeds as well as cooked rye berries for an even juicer texture. The loaf is hydrated completely with beer, and the miso content is pumped up to pack as much flavour as possible into every slice.

INGREDIENTS

RYE LEAVEN

100g	rye flour
100g	water
25g	Sourdough Starter (see pages 12–13)

DOUGH

160g	rye flour
260g	dark beer
160g	Rye Leaven (see above)
16g	malt syrup
80g	sunflower seeds, plus a handful for coating
25g	pumpkin seeds, plus a handful for coating
25g	sesame seeds, plus a handful for coating
16g	poppy seeds, plus a handful for coating
25g	brown flaxseed
25g	golden flaxseed
40g	ground flaxseed
8g	dark malt powder
24g	miso
32g	cooked rye berries
6g	salt

butter or oil, for greasing

METHOD

1. On day 1, combine all the rye leaven ingredients and place in a mixing bowl. Cover with a tea towel and let it ferment for 12 hours, or overnight.

2. The next day coat the inside of a loaf tin (pan) with butter or oil and set it aside. In a large bowl, combine all of the dough ingredients, and, using wet hands, mix together to form a thick dough with no dry flour remaining. Clean off and re-wet your hands to shape the dough into an oblong ball that's more or less the size of the loaf tin, but slightly narrower.

3. On a wide plate, combine the additional handfuls of sunflower, sesame, poppy and pumpkin seeds, then roll the loaf in the seeds so that it is well-coated on all sides.

4. Gently drop the loaf into the greased tin and set it aside in a warm place to ferment for 2–3 hours, placing it in a pan or bowl of warm water if necessary to bring the dough to 28°C (82.5°F). When it's ready to bake, the loaf will have risen slightly, and the top of the loaf should look slightly cracked.

(continued)

5. Preheat the oven to 220°C (425°F), Gas Mark 7. Have a rack in the centre of the oven. If you want to create steam, place a shallow roasting pan on the bottom shelf of the oven and let it heat with the oven.

6. Place the loaf in the oven, and if you are going for steam, add water to the roasting pan and quickly close the door.

7. Bake the loaf for 30 minutes, then rotate the tin, and bake for another 30 minutes, or until the internal temperature of the loaf is 95°C (203°F).

8. Remove the bread from the oven, then turn it out on to a rack to cool for several hours (ideally overnight) before slicing.

Makes
8 BAGELS

Everything Sourdough Bagels

This recipe is naturally leavened, meaning it requires a sourdough starter. To keep your starter active enough to get the volume and fermentation you want, you will need to feed the starter at least twice a day, about 12 hours apart, and then prepare your leaven from the starter a few hours before mixing the bagel dough.

INGREDIENTS

EVERYTHING SPICE

100g	sesame seeds
100g	poppy seeds
50g	caraway seeds
50g	mustard seeds
50g	nigella seeds
25g	sea salt flakes

LEAVEN

110g	warm water, at 90–100°C (195–210°F)
150g	ripe Sourdough Starter (see pages 12–13), just starting to collapse (should smell sweet with a little sourness, not vinegary yet)
75g	strong white bread flour (12–13% protein content)
25g	strong wholemeal flour

FINAL DOUGH

282g	water
104g	strong wholemeal flour
416g	strong white bread flour (12–13% protein content)
173g	Leaven (see above), just starting to collapse
39g	malted barley syrup

13g	salt

molasses (or malted barley syrup) and bicarbonate of soda (baking soda), for boiling

METHOD

1. To make the everything spice: in a mixing bowl, combine all ingredients and mix very well. This recipe will make extra; it keeps well indefinitely in a sealed container.

2. To make the leaven: mix all ingredients until all of the flour has been fully incorporated. It won't develop gluten, but there should be no clumps or bits of dry flour. Cover with a tea towel and leave in a warm place for 3–4 hours. It should ferment quickly and will be ready to use when it has fully risen, there are plenty of bubbles at the top, it smells sweet and slightly sour, and it just barely starts to collapse in the middle.

3. Combine all of the final dough ingredients in the bowl of a stand mixer fitted with a dough hook, then mix on speed 2 until everything comes together into a cohesive dough. Or if mixing by hand, mix together in a bowl until everything is fully incorporated. Cover and

let rest for about 15 minutes. This isn't a full autolyse; it just gives the flour some time to hydrate and will make mixing a bit easier.

4. After resting, mix until a smooth dough comes together. If mixing in a stand mixer, keep on speed 2 or 3, and mix for about 5–6 minutes. If mixing by hand, you may want to also knead directly on a clean surface for about 6–8 minutes.

5. When the dough is ready, it will have a nice spring to it when you poke it, it shouldn't feel sticky, and it should have a bit of a shine on the surface. Move the dough to a lightly oiled container and let it bulk ferment, covered, until the dough increases in volume by about 30–40%. The dough should start to get gassy and should feel stronger and more extensible. This will take roughly 3–4 hours but can change depending on a lot of variables like temperature, how active your leaven is, how fresh your flour is, etc.

6. The easiest way to determine how much volume your dough has gained during bulk fermentation is to use a clear container with straight walls so that you can mark the wall with a piece of tape to mark the height of the dough when you first put it in the container. Then you can use a ruler (or just eyeball it) to mark how much higher the dough needs to be to increase 30–40%.

7. When the dough has risen to the higher piece of tape, you are ready to divide. Once the dough has enough volume and is ready to divide, carefully tip it out of the container on to a clean surface. Using a bench scraper and a scale, divide the dough into 125g portions.

8. Once the dough has been divided, round each portion into a pretty tight boule. To do this, cup your hand around each portion of dough with your fingertips pressed to the surface of the counter and your palm touching the piece of dough. Rotate your hand in clockwise circles around the dough so that the bottom of the dough sticks to the surface, but the circular motion pinches the edges of the dough back underneath the ball of dough itself. You are trying to get a tight little ball of dough that doesn't immediately lose its shape.

9. Line a baking tray (sheet) with a piece of baking paper that has been lightly sprayed with nonstick spray. When all of the portions of dough have been pre-shaped into boules, place them on the tray. Don't put them so close to each other that they will stick together. Lightly spray them, cover them with clingfilm (plastic wrap) and place in the refrigerator overnight, ideally for 12–16 hours.

10. The following day, remove the dough balls from the refrigerator so they come back to room temperature. While waiting for the dough to temper, preheat your oven to 250°C (500°F), Gas Mark 10, and set the rack toward the top of your oven so that they colour evenly and don't burn on the bottoms while you bake them. If you have a pizza stone, put this in the oven during the preheating.

11. Bring a large, wide pot of water to a boil. You want the pot of water to be wide and shallow rather than narrow and deep so that you can fit in as many bagels as possible.

12. When the dough is room temperature, your water is boiling, and the oven is preheated, add about 2 tablespoons of molasses or malted barley syrup to the boiling water, and 1 teaspoon of bicarbonate of soda (baking soda).

13. Get your everything spice ready on a plate or a tray. You will also need a couple of baking trays (sheets) lined with nonstick baking paper and lightly sprayed with nonstick spray.

(continued)

14. To shape the bagels, use a finger to poke a hole right in the centre of the dough ball. Pick up the dough so that it fits around your finger like a ring, and gently stretch and rotate the dough around your finger over and over again until you have a bagel-sized ring with a hole in the middle of about 2.5–4cm (1–1½ inches) in diameter.

15. When the bagels have been shaped, gently and carefully place them into the boiling pot of water. Fit as many as you can at once so that an even layer floats on the top, close to each other but not touching. Boil for 1 minute, then carefully flip on to the other side. Boil for another minute, then remove the bagels one-by-one from the water using a slotted spoon or skimmer and place the top (smooth) side directly into the everything spice.

16. The bagels will have gotten about 50% bigger during the boiling process. Gently shake the bagel around in the everything spice so that it gets coated very well. Move each bagel to the lined trays, and repeat until they have all been boiled and rolled in everything spice.

17. Once the bagels are all boiled and coated with the spice mixture, make sure they are evenly spaced on the trays, spice-side up, so that they don't touch while baking. Keep in mind they will still rise a bit more in the oven. Bake all of the bagels in the oven for 8 minutes.

18. Rotate the trays so that the bagels bake evenly, and bake for another 4–6 minutes depending on how dark you like your bagels to be.

19. Pull the bagels from the oven, and move them to a cooling rack so that they can cool completely.

Rosemary Focaccia

INGREDIENTS

SPONGE

800ml	water
500g	strong white bread flour
7g	fast-action (active) dried yeast

DOUGH

500g	00 flour
20g	fine sea salt
30ml	extra virgin olive oil, plus extra for greasing
5g	caster (superfine) sugar

TOPPING

80ml	extra virgin olive oil
4	rosemary sprigs, chopped
sea salt flakes	

METHOD

1. Whisk together the water and bread flour with the dried yeast. Cover and leave in a warm place until the sponge is full of bubbles.

2. Place the 00 flour into a large bowl with the fine sea salt, olive oil and sugar. With your hands, slowly incorporate the sponge mixture into the bowl with the other ingredients until well combined with no signs of flour.

3. With wet hands, place the dough in a well-oiled container, and leave for 1 hour.

4. Stretch and fold the dough (see page 26, step 8) and repeat once more. Place in the refrigerator overnight.

5. The next day, with wet hands, gently remove the dough and place on a well-oiled baking tray (sheet). Give the dough a book fold (folding one side into the middle and then folding the opposite side on top) and then cover and leave to rise until doubled in size.

6. Preheat the oven to 220°C (425°F), Gas Mark 7.

7. Once the dough has doubled in size, uncover and gently rub brush with the 80ml of olive oil and the chopped rosemary, and sprinkle the sea salt all over the surface. Dimple the surface with your fingers.

8. Place the focaccia in the oven and bake for about 25 minutes, until golden brown.

100% Rye Sourdough

INGREDIENTS

LEAVEN

75g	Rye Sourdough Starter (see pages 12–13)
110g	dark rye flour
150g	tepid water

DOUGH

150g	Rye flour, plus extra for sprinkling (optional)
5g	salt
1 tsp each	caraway, fennel aniseed (anise seeds) or coriander seed, or to taste
335g	Leaven (see above)
110g	hot water (just below boiling)

1 heaped tbsp black treacle or molasses
sprinkle of seeds – sunflower, linseed, pumpkin seeds (optional)

butter, for greasing

METHOD

1. Make the leaven 5 hours before you add to the dough to allow the leaven to mature (see pages 12–13). Mix the ingredients together in a bowl and cover.

2. Mix the rye flour, salt and spices together. Put the leaven in a bowl and sprinkle the rye flour mix evenly on top to cover the leaven.

3. Add the hot water to the treacle and mix together. Pour the treacle and water mix over the flour and slowly mix the treacle water into the flour layer, leaving the leaven underneath undisturbed until it cools down, so as not to damage the leaven.

4. Mix it all together to a thick paste and scrape into a well-buttered 450g (1lb) loaf tin. Evenly press down the mixture and smooth over the top with the back of a wet spoon. Sprinkle a little rye flour or seeds on top.

5. Allow to ferment for about 2 hours in a warm environment, ideally 25–30°C (77–86°). (You can use your oven as a proving place: turn it on a low heat for 5 minutes and then turn off). The dough has proved enough when it has almost reached the tin rim and cracks have appeared on the surface.

6. Preheat the oven to 240°C (475°F), Gas Mark 9.

7. Bake in the oven for about 40 minutes, taking the loaf out of the tin for the last 10 minutes. The internal temperature should be 98°C (208°F).

SAVOURY BAKES

Makes
4 LARGE or 6 SMALL FLATBREADS

Lahm bi Ajeen

Lahm bi ajeen (literally 'meat with dough') is a popular Levantine, Turkish (*lahmaçun*) and Armenian (*lamadjo*) spiced, meat-topped flatbread. It's sometimes called Turkish pizza or Lebanese pizza, but in this part of the world the act of cooking topped flatbreads in an oven predates Italian pizza by centuries. This recipe works for both a home oven and a pizza oven; the only difference is it needs a few minutes longer in a home oven as it can't get as hot.

INGREDIENTS

DOUGH

150ml	lukewarm water
250g	strong white bread flour, plus extra for dusting
3g	fast-action (active) dried yeast
6g	fine salt
splash of olive oil	

TOPPING AND GARNISH

2	tomatoes
1½	small red onions
3	garlic cloves
60g	parsley, plus a few sprigs to garnish
200g	lamb mince
1 tbsp	tomato purée (paste)
1 tbsp	hot pepper paste
1 tsp	salt, plus a pinch to garnish
100g	butter
4 tbsp	pomegranate molasses
1	lemon, juice only

METHOD

1. In a stand mixer, combine the water and flour and mix for a minute until just combined. Leave to sit for 30 minutes to autolyse, then add the yeast and mix for a few minutes. Add the salt and oil and mix again until smooth and elastic. Probably about 10 minutes total mixing time.

2. Remove the dough, shape into a ball and place into a clean bowl. Cover and leave until doubled in size, around 1 hour.

3. Once the dough has risen, transfer to a lightly floured surface and divide into 4 large or 6 smaller pieces. Shape each piece into a ball and then cover and leave to rest for 30 minutes.

4. While the dough rests, preheat the oven (or a pizza oven) to 250°C (500°F), Gas Mark 10.

5. Make the topping: core and deseed the tomatoes and then finely chop along with 1 of the onions, the garlic and 30g of the parsley. It should be really fine; the easiest way to do this is to stick it all in a food processor and blitz it.

(continued)

6. Add the mix to a large bowl along with the lamb mince, tomato and red pepper paste and the teaspoon of salt. Mix really well. Cook off a small chunk in a hot pan to taste for seasoning.

7. Before cooking, get the garnish ready. Melt the butter in a small saucepan until it just starts to brown. Finely chop the remaining 30g of parsley, add to the butter (it will spit a little, so be careful) and turn off the heat.

8. In a small bowl, combine the pomegranate molasses, lemon juice and pinch of salt. Mix and set aside. Finely slice the remaining half red onion and set aside.

9. Roll out each ball of dough into a very thin circle, about about 2mm ($\frac{1}{16}$ inch) thick. Add a thin layer of the lamb mix and spread using your fingertips, gently pushing it into the dough, until the whole surface is covered.

10. Cook in a pizza oven for about 2 minutes until crispy and golden, or in a home oven on a baking tray (sheet) for about 5–6 minutes.

11. Remove from the oven, drizzle over a spoonful of the parsley butter and a spoonful of the pomegranate sauce. Finish with a few sprigs of fresh parsley and some slivers of red onion. Roll up and enjoy.

Batbout Buns with Berber Omelette

INGREDIENTS

BATBOUT BUNS

250g	organic self-raising white flour
1 tsp	sea salt flakes
250g	live natural (plain) yogurt

BERBER OMELETTE (MAKES 1)

1 tbsp	olive oil
½	small onion, thinly sliced
½ tsp	ground cumin
½ tsp	ground coriander
2	eggs, well beaten
½ tsp	finely chopped mint
½ tsp	finely chopped coriander
¼ tsp	fine sea salt
1 tbsp	spicy harissa (optional)

METHOD

BATBOUT BUNS

1. Preheat the oven to 220°C (425°F), Gas Mark 7 and line a baking tray (sheet) with nonstick baking paper.

2. Sift the flour into a bowl with the salt. Add the yogurt and bring everything together using your hands until well combined and no flour is visible.

3. Divide the dough into 5 × 100g balls and flatten them by hand into 10cm (4-inch) rounds. Batbout buns are meant to be rustic, so do not get caught up with using a rolling pin or trying to shape them perfectly.

4. Place the rounds on the lined tray and bake for 8 minutes, flipping them over halfway through the cooking time.

5. Meanwhile, preheat a ridged griddle pan. Take the buns out of the oven and place each one on the hot pan. Check after 2 minutes and when the buns have those blackened grill lines, flip them over to achieve this on both sides.

BERBER OMELETTE

1. Heat the olive oil in a heavy-based frying pan.

(continued)

2. Add the onion and fry for 3 minutes.

3. Add the spices and cook over a low heat for a further 5 minutes. Add the beaten eggs, chopped herbs and salt. This is not like a traditional omelette, so you can vigorously stir the mixture until just cooked.

4. Split open a batbout bun and pack in the omelette. We serve ours with a tablespoon of spicy harissa on top of the omelette.

Leila Tang

Cheese & Miso Rolls

During the 1970s my parents lived as refugees in Hong Kong. There, Mum and Dad noticed many bakeries filled with mouthwatering displays of soft, fluffy buns in all different shapes and flavours, but they could not afford to buy any of them. After my parents settled in the UK, they were eventually able to enjoy Hong-Kong-style buns from Chinatown, London. Since then, we have made many more at home! This recipe, which has our own little twist on it, takes inspiration from Chinese bakeries that often combine sweet and savoury flavours in the same bite.

INGREDIENTS

220g	full-fat (whole) milk
20g	fresh yeast
100g	white miso paste
450g	strong white bread flour, plus extra for dusting
100g	caster (superfine) sugar
50g	unsalted butter, softened
240g	mature Cheddar, grated
2	spring onions, finely chopped

METHOD

1. Gently warm the milk in a saucepan to body temperature. Remove the saucepan from the heat and dissolve the yeast in the milk.

2. To make the dough, place the miso paste in a mixing bowl with the flour, sugar and butter, then add the milk and yeast. Using a scraper, combine the ingredients in the bowl, then transfer the dough to a work surface and knead for 20 minutes until smooth and elastic. Or, if using a stand mixer, knead using the dough hook.

3. Shape the dough into a ball and place it back in the mixing bowl. Leave it to rest for 2 hours, covered with a cloth in a warm place at approx. 36°C (97°F).

4. After the dough has proved, transfer it to a lightly floured work surface. Using a rolling pin, roll the dough into a rectangle about 50 × 40cm (20 × 16 inches), keeping a long edge closest to you.

(continued)

5. Sprinkle the grated cheese and chopped spring onion on to the rectangle of dough, leaving a 1.5cm (⅝-inch) clear strip on the bottom and top edges. Brush these strips with a little water, and then roll up from the side closest to you. Once you have formed a log, divide into 10 equal-sized portions with a knife.

6. Line a baking tray (sheet) with nonstick baking paper. Transfer the rolls to the tray with the flat, circular side down so that the rolls stand vertically on the tray. Allow enough space between each roll for proving. Leave to prove in a warm place for 2 hours.

7. Preheat the oven to 170°C (335°F), Gas Mark 3.

8. Bake the proved rolls for 20 minutes. These buns will keep for up to 2 days but are best enjoyed fresh.

Olive Oil Buns

INGREDIENTS

180g	water
180g	full-fat (whole) milk
2	eggs
30g	fresh yeast or 10g fast-action (active) dried yeast
750g	T65 (French white bread) flour, plus extra for dusting
22g	fine sea salt
22g	caster (superfine) sugar
90g	extra virgin olive oil
1	egg, beaten, to glaze

METHOD

1. Gently warm the water and milk to room temperature and place in a stand mixer. Add the eggs and yeast followed by the remaining dry ingredients. Mix on a low speed for 5 minutes.

2. Using a dough scraper, clean down the inside of the mixing bowl and let the dough rest for 5 minutes. Pour in the olive oil and mix on medium speed for 5 minutes, then clean down the sides of the mixing bowl again with the dough scraper. Mix on low speed for a further 5 minutes.

3. Transfer the dough to a floured work surface, scrape it into a tight ball and place in a container or bowl with enough room for it to comfortably double in size. Cover and leave for 1 hour, when it should have doubled in size; f not, wait a while longer.

4. Line a baking tray (sheet) with nonstick baking paper. Portion the dough into 100g pieces, then roll into balls and space out evenly on the lined tray. Cover and prove for 1 hour or until doubled in size.

5. Preheat the oven to 185°C (365°F), Gas Mark 4.

6. Once proved, glaze the buns with the eggwash and bake for 10–14 minutes.

7. When cool, greedily stuff with mortadella, burrata and pistachio pesto (or whichever filling you desire!).

Kevan Roberts

Makes
1 LOAF

Spring Onion & Brie Sourdough

INGREDIENTS

390g	strong white bread flour
78g	active, mature Sourdough Starter (see pages 12–13)
280g	water, at around 26°C (79°F)
8g	salt
oil, for greasing	
75g	spring onions, chopped with one left whole
75g	Brie

METHOD

DAY 1

1. Place the flour in a bowl. In a separate bowl, add the sourdough starter to the water, and break down the starter into the water. Using your hands, combine this with the flour to make a dough. Then cover and leave to rest for 30 minutes.

2. Add the salt with a couple of spritzes of water to aid the dissolving of the salt. Bring everything together to form a dough, then knead and develop by hand for 10 minutes.

3. Or, if using a stand mixer, mix on a slow speed with the hook attachment for 2 minutes, then on a fast speed for 6 minutes.

4. Once mixed, place in a lightly oiled bowl and give the dough a fold. To do this, stretch and fold all corners of the dough over (see page 26, step 8). Leave for 45 minutes, then give a second fold. Leave for 45 minutes again, then give a third fold; and then leave for a further 45 minutes.

5. Now it's time to add your extras. This is more of a gentle affair and don't get this confused with kneading: stretch your dough out into a pizza shape and place the chopped spring onions and Brie on top, breaking the cheese into thumbnail-size pieces. Fold the top

(continued)

of the dough to meet the bottom, resembling a pasty, and then apply pressure with the heel of your hand to push the dough and fold. Keep doing this until your inclusions are evenly distributed. Cover and leave for 45 minutes.

6. Pre-shape the dough into a ball. Place on a lightly oiled surface, cover and leave for 30 minutes.

7. To shape the bread, you will need a round proving basket heavily dusted with flour. Split in half a large spring onion and place this into the bottom of your proving basket.

8. Take your dough and turn upside down, bring all the corners over to meet in the middle, then stitch the dough together down the middle. Turn over and bring together to form a ball, and then place in your floured basket, seam-side up.

9. Leave at room temperature for 2 hours. Then place into the refrigerator for 12–18 hours.

DAY 2

10. Preheat the oven 250°C (500°F), Gas Mark 10. For best results place a cast-iron pot large enough to fit the dough into the oven to heat up. Or place a baking tray (sheet) in the oven to heat.

11. If baking in the pot, take the pot out of the oven, place the dough in the pot and slash a square on top. Place the lid on the pot and bake for 30 minutes. Take off the lid and bake for a further 10 minutes.

12. If baking on a tray, take the tray out of the oven, place the bread on top, then slash a square on top of the loaf. Place in the oven with a small container of water to add some steam. Bake for 30 minutes.

13. Take out of the oven. Allow to cool and serve with the finest butter you have: this beauty deserves it!

Leek, Guanciale & Pecorino Quiche

INGREDIENTS

PASTRY

250g	strong white bread flour, plus extra for dusting
200g	unsalted butter, cubed
3g	fine sea salt
50g	ice-cold water

FILLING

9	large eggs
300ml	full-fat (whole) milk
90ml	double (heavy) cream
9g	fine sea salt
nutmeg, for grating	
180g	guanciale, cut into generous lardons
2	leeks, cut into rounds
60g	Pecorino Romano, finely grated
90g	Gruyère, coarsely grated
handful of finely chopped chives	
black pepper	

METHOD

1. For the pastry, combine the flour, butter and salt in the bowl of a stand mixer. Place the whole lot in the refrigerator for 30 minutes until very cold.

2. Using the paddle attachment, mix the butter and flour on the lowest speed until the mixture has the texture of coarse breadcrumbs. Now, slowly trickle in the water until the mix comes together into a smooth, homogeneous dough. Turn the dough out onto a lightly floured surface and very briefly knead until completely smooth. Wrap loosely in clingfilm (plastic wrap) and shape into a flat disc. Wrap the clingfilm tightly around the pastry and chill for at least 45 minutes, ideally overnight.

3. Once rested, roll the pastry out on a lightly floured surface until roughly 3mm (1/8 inch) thick and large enough to line a deep 20cm (8-inch) springform cake tin (pan) with plenty of overhang. Lower the pastry gently into the tin and press against the sides, along the base and right into the corners. Pop it back into the refrigerator for another 30–45 minutes.

4. Meanwhile, preheat the oven to 200°C (400°F), Gas Mark 6.

(continued)

5. Combine the eggs, milk, cream and salt with a few twists of pepper and plenty of grated nutmeg in a large bowl. Using a hand blender or whisk, mix until completely smooth: this is your quiche custard. Set aside.

6. Add the guanciale to a large frying pan over a medium heat and cook until the guanciale is crisp and completely rendered. Remove from the pan, leaving the fat behind.

7. Add the leeks to the pan and sweat down in the guanciale fat until soft and bright green. Toss through the crispy guanciale and set aside.

8. Line the pastry case with aluminium foil, fill with baking beans and blind bake for 20–25 minutes.

9. Remove the foil and bake for a further 10–15 minutes until golden brown. Turn the oven down to 170°C (335°F), Gas Mark 3.

10. Spoon the leeks and guanciale into the baked pastry, scatter over both cheeses and pour over the quiche custard. Cover with a blanket of chopped chives and return to the oven for 60–70 minutes until just set with a tiny wobble in the middle.

11. Cut away the excess pastry using a serrated knife and allow to cool for 2 hours.

12. Now remove your quiche from the tin, slice and serve warm. This is delicious with a simple green salad and a good chutney.

Pissaladière

INGREDIENTS

DOUGH

200g   cold unsalted butter, cut into cubes
300g   plain (all-purpose) flour
½ tsp   fine salt
pinch of granulated sugar
100ml   iced water

TOPPING

6   large red onions, thinly sliced
olive oil, for frying and drizzling
20   anchovy fillets (we use salted Ortiz,
         which we rinse and fillet)
140g   black niçoise olives
bunch of fresh thyme, chopped
sea salt flakes
cracked black pepper

METHOD

1. Start by making the dough: using a food processor, bring together the butter, flour, salt and sugar until it resembles fine breadcrumbs. Slowly add the iced water, a little at a time, until the dough barely comes together.

2. Wrap the dough in clingfilm (plastic wrap) and chill for 2–3 hours before using. (This can be made a couple of days in advance and will keep in the refrigerator.)

3. To make the topping, in a large, wide, heavy-based saucepan, gently sweat the onions in a little olive oil with some sea salt flakes and cracked black pepper, covered with a cartouche (a circle of baking paper folded into segments then unfolded, crumpled and dampened), until the onions are soft; this should take 1 hour.

4. When the onions are soft, remove the cartouche to evaporate the excess liquid. Do not allow the onions to colour – they should be soft and intensely sweet but not caramelized. Remove from the pan and leave to cool.

5. Line a 28 × 43cm (11 × 17-inch) baking tray (sheet), then using a box grater, grate the cold pastry on to the tray. Grating breaks up the gluten strands, which gives you a much thinner crust.

(continued)

6. Then press the dough into the base to form a thin layer along the bottom of the tray.

7. Cover again and chill for a further 30 minutes.

8. Meanwhile, preheat the oven to 160°C (325°C), Gas Mark 3.

9. Remove the tray from the refrigerator and prick the base a couple of times with a fork. Bake in the oven for 40 minutes until crisp but not browned.

10. Remove the crust from the oven and allow to cool slightly.

11. Top with the onions and smooth out to form a thin layer. Lattice the anchovies across the top of the onions and place an olive in each square. Sprinkle with thyme, black pepper and olive oil and bake in the oven for a further 20 minutes.

12. Pack in your picnic basket, along with fresh greens for a salad and a bottle of Domaine Tempier rosé. Enjoy!

Cheddar, Anchovy & Rosemary Scones

INGREDIENTS

450g	plain (all-purpose) flour, plus extra for dusting
30g	baking powder
100g	butter, cubed
1 tsp	sea salt flakes, plus extra for garnishing
1 tsp	freshly ground pepper
100g	mature Cheddar, roughly grated
100g	Parmesan, finely grated
500g	buttermilk or natural (plain) yogurt
½ tsp	very finely chopped rosemary, plus a few sprigs to garnish
6–8	anchovy fillets, finely chopped

a little milk, for brushing

METHOD

1. Heat the oven to 180°C (350°F), Gas Mark 4. Line a baking tray (sheet) with nonstick baking paper.

2. Place the flour, baking powder and butter in a large bowl with the salt and pepper and mix. Rub the butter into the dry ingredients until the mixture resembles medium crumbs.

3. Add the cheeses, buttermilk or yogurt, rosemary and the anchovy fillets. then mix with a fork until everything comes together. Very gently knead the dough together in the bowl, then tip it out on to a lightly floured board. Shape into a flat disc, approx. 30cm (12 inches) across and 4cm (1½ inches) thick.

4. Place the disc of dough on the lined baking tray (sheet), then brush all over with the milk. Using the long handle of a wooden spoon, create a criss-cross of indentations over the top to mark out 10 triangles pressing no more than half the way into the dough. Garnish each portion with the rosemary sprigs and sprinkle with sea salt.

5. Bake for 35–45 minutes or until puffed and golden brown, turning halfway through the cooking time for even baking.

6. Serve as soon as possible, cutting along the indentations. Serve with butter and a soup or salad.

SWEET DOUGH

Crème Diplomat Filled Doughnuts

INGREDIENTS

CREME DIPLOMAT

400g	full-fat (whole) milk
180g	double (heavy) cream
150g	caster (superfine) sugar
1	vanilla pod (bean), seeds scraped
125g	egg yolk
40g	cornflour (cornstarch)

DOUGHNUTS

200g	full-fat (whole) milk
30g	fresh yeast
2	large eggs
500g	flour (W95 / P/L 0,22), plus extra for dusting
100g	caster (superfine) sugar
90g	cold butter, cut into cubes
½ tsp	salt

neutral oil, for deep-frying
caster (superfine) or icing (confectioners')
    sugar, for coating

METHOD

CREME DIPLOMAT

1. In a heavy-based saucepan on very low heat, bring the milk, 100g of the double (heavy) cream, half the caster (superfine) sugar and the scraped seeds of the vanilla pod (bean) together with the pod to a very gentle simmer.

2. While you're waiting for the milk mixture to simmer, mix the egg yolk, remaining 75g caster (superfine) sugar and the cornflour (cornstarch) in a bowl and whisk for a couple of minutes to incorporate a little air in the mix.

3. When the milk starts to simmer, slowly pour the warm mixture into the egg yolk mix while whisking constantly to prevent curdling.

4. Strain the mixture back to the saucepan and cook over a low–medium heat, constantly whisking for about 10 minutes, or until it starts to slowly simmer and become very thick.

5. Transfer the cream to a shallow container and place a sheet of clingfilm (plastic wrap) directly on the surface of the custard. Leave to cool, then chill in the refrigerator for 4–5 hours or overnight.

(continued)

DOUGHNUTS

1. In the bowl of a stand mixer, fitted with a dough hook, mix the milk, fresh yeast and eggs until the yeast has dissolved.

2. Add the flour and sugar and mix on medium speed until the dough comes together and pulls away from the sides of the bowl.

3. Add the cold butter and salt and mix on medium–high speed until the butter is incorporated and the dough is smooth, very elastic and comes away from the sides of the bowl.

4. Place the dough in a greased container and leave to rise in a warm place for about 1½ hours or until it has doubled in size.

5. While the dough is rising, cut about 16 10cm (4 inch) squares of baking paper.

6. On a lightly floured surface, take the dough out of the container, then cut the dough into 60g pieces (you should get about 16 pieces).

7. Roll each piece into a very tight ball by bringing all sides of the dough into the centre, then turning it around and rolling with the palm of your hand on the work surface.

8. Place each ball on the prepared baking paper squares, seam-side down, and leave to rise for about 30–45 minutes or until very puffy and doubled in size.

9. While the doughnuts are proving, fill a heavy-based saucepan halfway with the oil and heat to 160°C (325°F).

10. When the oil is heated and the doughnuts are proved, working in batches, carefully slip 2–3 doughnuts (depending on the size on your pan) into the oil using the paper to help you. If the paper falls in the pan, remove it with tongs.

11. Fry the doughnuts on both sides for a couple of minutes until golden brown on each side. You should get a white stripe in the middle of your doughnuts if they have risen properly!

12. Remember to constantly check the oil temperature and try to keep it at 160°C (325°F); that way they won't absorb too much oil and they'll cook properly in the middle without getting too brown.

13. Using tongs, remove the doughnuts from the oil, letting the excess oil drip back into the pan, then place them on kitchen paper.

14. At this point, while they are still warm, you can coat them with caster (superfine) sugar, then let them cool down before filling them. Alternatively, you could let them cool down first, fill them up with the crème diplomat and then coat them with icing (confectioners') sugar.

ASSEMBLY

15. Make a hole with a small pointy knife in the crease of each doughnut before filling.

16. To finish the crème diplomat, whip the remaining 80g of double (heavy) cream to soft peaks, being careful not to overwhip. Then fold into the custard until fully incorporated and lusciously creamy.

17. Fill a piping (pastry) bag with your crème diplomat and get on filling the doughnuts!

Far Breton

INGREDIENTS

200g	prunes, pitted
50g	rum
50g	unsalted, melted butter
130g	caster (superfine) sugar
4	eggs
110g	plain (all-purpose) flour
pinch of salt	
750g	cold full-fat (whole) milk

METHOD

1. Soak the prunes in the rum for at least a few hours, or overnight if time allows.

2. Preheat the oven to 240°C (475°F), Gas Mark 9.

3. Grease a 4cm- (1½-inch)-deep 20 × 25cm (8 × 10-inch), or equivalent, oval earthenware dish with the melted butter.

4. Spoon the soaked prunes into your buttered dish, and then put it into the oven for a few minutes just to warm up the prunes.

5. Mix the sugar and eggs together until pale and gradually add the flour, then the salt. Slowly whisk in the cold milk to make a thin batter. Remove the dish from the oven and pour in the batter. Bake in the oven for 10 minutes, then turn down the heat to 200°C (400°F), Gas Mark 6, and bake for a further 25–30 minutes.

6. To check the Far is ready, dip the blade of a sharp knife into cold water, and then use it to pierce the middle – if the knife comes out clean, it is ready. The sides of the Far will also be starting to come away from the dish.

7. Cool completely in the dish and then slice into pieces or use a round cutter.

8. Serve with a cup of tea and a rum-soaked prune dipped in chocolate!

Layla's Cocoa Hot Cross Buns

INGREDIENTS

TANGZHONG

115g	water
115g	full-fat (whole) milk
35g	strong white bread flour

BUNS

590g	strong white bread flour
50g	(unsweetened) cocoa powder
100g	soft light brown sugar
1 tsp	ground ginger
1 tsp	ground cardamom
1 tsp	sea salt flakes
250g	full-fat (whole) milk
2	eggs
30g	fresh yeast
120g	unsalted butter, at room temperature
100g	raisins
100g	candied orange peel
100g	dark (semisweet) chocolate chips

TO FINISH

100g	strong white bread flour
75g	water
3	eggs, for eggwash

orange marmalade, for glazing

METHOD

1. Start by making the tangzhong: in a pan over medium heat, whisk together the water, milk and flour until it has the consistency of double (heavy) cream. Then let it cool down.

2. Next, add all the dry bun ingredients to the bowl of a stand mixer and mix for 5 minutes at a slow speed, then add the cooled tangzhong, milk, eggs and yeast.

3. Mix for 10 minutes, then start adding the butter in small pieces little by little, increasing the speed as you go until the mixture detaches from the sides.

4. Add the dried fruits and chocolate chips and mix through for 2 minutes. Take out of the mixer, place in an oiled bowl and cover with clingfilm (plastic wrap).

5. Let the mixture prove at room temperature for 1½ hours, or put it in the refrigerator overnight.

6. Line a tray with nonstick baking paper and scale the dough into 70g balls, arranging the buns 3cm (1¼ inches) apart on the lined tray. Let the buns prove on the tray for another hour at room temperature.

7. Preheat the oven to 170°C (335°F), Gas Mark 3.

(continued)

8. While the buns are proving, make the cross mix by combining with a whisk the bread flour and water, adding the water little by little.

9. Whisk the eggs together to create your eggwash, then brush this over the buns.

10. Transfer the cross mix to a piping (pastry) bag and pipe the cross on to the buns.

11. Bake for 15 minutes. Turn the tray around and then bake for a further 5 minutes.

12. Glaze with orange marmalade once out of the oven, using a brush.

Passion Fruit & Yuzu Choux Buns

INGREDIENTS

PASSION FRUIT & YUZU CURD

300g	passion fruit juice
100g	candied yuzu, finely chopped
200g	egg (shelled weight)
250g	egg yolk
500g	caster (superfine) sugar
700g	unsalted butter, diced

CRAQUELIN TOPPING

30g	unsalted butter, softened
30g	soft light brown sugar
10g	whipping cream
30g	plain (all-purpose) flour

CHOUX PASTRY

125ml	water
60g	unsalted butter
15g	caster (superfine) sugar
75g	strong white bread flour
2	egg yolks, at room temperature

METHOD

1. To make the passion fruit and yuzu curd, add all the ingredients except the butter to a saucepan and stir over a low heat for 10 minutes.

2. Slowly whisk in the butter, just like you would when making mayonnaise, until the mix is thick and shiny. Remove from the heat, leave to cool down and then set in the refrigerator.

3. To make the craquelin topping, place the soft butter in a bowl and beat with a spatula to make sure there are no lumps, then add the brown sugar and cream. Then add the flour to make a smooth paste.

4. Place the craquelin dough between two sheets of nonstick baking paper. Gently flatten with your hands and then roll to 4mm (⅛ inch) thick. Place in the freezer for 2 hours.

5. Preheat the oven to 180°C (350°C), Gas Mark 4.

6. To make the choux pastry, place a saucepan on a medium heat with the water, butter and sugar. Heat until the butter is melted and the sugar is dissolved.

7. Remove from the heat, then add the flour in one go and mix with a spatula to form a rough dough. Put the pan back on the heat and beat

(continued)

for 3 minutes until smooth. Add the egg yolks, one at a time, beating after each one.

8. Line several baking trays (sheets) with nonstick baking paper. Transfer the choux pastry to a piping (pastry) bag and pipe the choux into balls 3cm (1¼ inches) apart on the lined trays.

9. Take the craquelin out of the freezer. Remove the top piece of paper and cut out rounds the same size as the choux buns. Using an offset spatula, place a craquelin disc on each choux bun.

10. Bake for 20 minutes, then reduce the heat to 160°C (325°C), Gas Mark 3, and bake for a further 10 minutes until puffed up, golden brown and dry to touch.

11. Leave to cool down completely on a cooling rack.

12. To finish, make a small hole in the bottom of the choux pastry and pipe the passion fruit and yuzu curd into the choux buns.

Marcelo Martins
LITTLE BREAD PEDLAR

Potato Sweet Brioche

INGREDIENTS

300g	cooked floury (baking) potatoes
250g	eggs, plus 1 egg, beaten, for the egg wash
250g	full-fat (whole) milk
200g	caster (superfine) sugar
25g	fresh yeast or 1 sachet of fast-action (active) dried yeast
1kg	strong white bread flour
10g	fine sea salt
250g	unsalted butter, softened

TO DECORATE

400ml	sugar syrup, for glazing (60% caster /superfine sugar and 40% water)
200g	desiccated coconut (optional)

METHOD

1. In a blender, combine the cooked potato, eggs, milk, sugar and yeast. Blend it till homogenized.

2. Transfer to a bowl and add the flour, then start kneading till the dough feels strong. Add the salt and butter and finish kneading till the dough feels strong and smooth.

3. Leave for 1 hour, allowing the dough to double in size, then divide into 20–26 balls, of roughly 90g each.

4. Once you finish dividing, start stretching them into strands long enough to make simple knots.

5. Space the knots on trays ready to prove. Cover with a tea towel and leave in a warm place for 40 minutes to 1 hour.

6. Preheat the oven to 190°C (375°F), Gas Mark 5.

7. Eggwash the knots and bake them for 20–25 minutes.

8. Glaze them with a simple sugar syrup. You could also scatter over some desiccated coconut (optional).

Cardamom Buns (Cardi B)

INGREDIENTS

DOUGH

500g	lukewarm water
30g	fresh yeast
500g	wholemeal spelt flour
15g	fine sea salt
400g	caster (superfine) sugar
3	eggs
15g	ground cardamom seeds
900g	strong stoneground white bread flour
200g	unsalted butter, softened and cubed

FILLING

400g	unsalted butter, at room temperature
150g	caster (superfine) sugar
150g	soft dark brown sugar
5g	fine sea salt
15g	ground cardamom seeds

LEMON SUGAR SYRUP

200g	caster (superfine) sugar
8 tbsp	lemon juice (from 2 lemons)
100g	cold water
2	eggs, beaten, for eggwash

METHOD

1. In the bowl of a stand mixer fitted with the dough hook, mix together all the dough ingredients apart from the butter. Mix for approx. 10 minutes, then rest for 20 minutes.

2. Slowly add the butter. Once all the butter is incorporated into the dough, mix for 10 minutes on a medium speed. Then cover and rest for a further 30 minutes.

3. While the dough is resting, mix together the butter filling. Put all the ingredients, except the ground cardamom, in the bowl of a stand mixer fitted with a balloon whisk – or a hand whisk will do – and mix until all the ingredients are combined. Set aside.

4. Now it is time to roll the dough out; roll it into a rectangular shape, approx. 40cm (16 inches) long and 60cm (24 inches) wide.

5. Cover the dough with the butter filling and sprinkle with the ground cardamom. Now you need to fold down the top edge of the dough about ⅔ over the butter filling, and then fold the bottom edge of the dough up to the middle of the dough.

6. You then need to roll the dough to about 30cm (12 inches) long and 40cm (16 inches) wide.

(continued)

7. Next you need to cut the dough:
I recommend using a pizza slicer for this and a
rolling pin for a ruler. Cut from bottom to the
top of the dough, cutting 2cm (¾-inch) slices
(approx. 100g) all along the shaped rectangle.
Remember to use your rolling pin as your
ruler to keep straight lines.

8. For shaping the buns, twist the long strip
of dough, by holding one end still on the work
surface and with your other hand rolling the
dough away from you; this will twist the dough.
Then wrap the twisted dough around your
index finger and your ring finger to create the
shape of the bun, and then tuck the end of the
twist into the centre of the bun.

9. Pop on to a baking tray (sheet) lined with
nonstick baking paper and cover with a light
tea towel, then allow to prove for approx.
2–2½ hours in a warm environment.

10. For baking, preheat your oven to 200°C
(400°F), Gas Mark 6.

11. Eggwash your buns, then bake in the
middle of the oven for approx. 20 minutes.

12. While they are baking, make up the lemon
sugar syrup, as you want to put this warm on
your buns when they come out the oven: in a
deep pan, mix together the sugar, lemon juice
and water with a wooden spoon. Put the pan
over a medium heat, and allow the mix to
come to the boil.

13. Once boiling leave over a medium heat for
2 minutes, and then allow to rest on the side.

14. Once the buns are golden, take them out
of the oven. Brush on a generous amount of
your warm lemon syrup with a pastry brush
and let the buns soak up the zesty syrup. At
Flori, we serve the buns warm all morning and
recommend pairing the bun with a caramel-
noted coffee bean.

YQ Aniseed Buns

INGREDIENTS

DOUGH

30g	oat milk
90g	unsalted butter
20g	finely ground aniseed (anise seeds)
250g	strong white bread flour
250g	YQ flour
12g	fast-action (active) dried yeast
1	egg
75g	caster (superfine) sugar
10g	salt

FILLING

180g	butter
120g	muscovado sugar
15g	salt
8g	finely ground aniseed (anise seeds)
2	eggs, beaten, for eggwash

METHOD

1. The night before making the dough, chill all the ingredients in the refrigerator.

2. The next day place all the dough ingredients in the bowl of a stand mixer with a dough hook. Mix on a medium speed for 4 minutes until properly incorporated.

3. Stop the machine and allow the dough to rest for 5 minutes. Then mix again on speed 2 for 4 minutes.

4. Divide into 2 ball. Cover them up with a tea towel and let them rest until the next day in the refrigerator.

5. The next day, preheat the oven to 170°C (335°F), Gas Mark 3.

6. Put the butter, sugar and salt in the bowl of a stand mixer and allow them to sit together until they become room temperature. Place the bowl in the stand mixer with the paddle attachment and mix until all combined.

7. Now you need to roll the dough out: roll into a 1cm thick rectangular shape. Cover the dough with the butter filling and sprinkle with the ground aniseed.

(continued)

8. Now fold down the top edge of the dough about ⅔ over the butter filling, and then fold the bottom edge of the dough up to the middle.

9. You then need to roll the dough to about 30cm (12 inches) long and 40cm (16 inches) wide.

10. Next you need to cut the dough: I recommend using a pizza slicer for this and a rolling pin for a ruler. Cut from bottom to the top of the dough, cutting 2cm (¾-inch) slices (approx. 100g) all along the shaped rectangle. Remember to use your rolling pin as your ruler to keep straight lines.

11. For shaping the buns, twist the long strip of dough by holding one end still on the work surface and with your other hand rolling the dough away from you; this will twist the dough. Then wrap the twisted dough around your index finger and your ring finger to create the shape of the bun, and then tuck the end of the twist into the centre of the bun.

12. Pop on to a baking tray (sheet) lined with nonstick baking paper and cover with a light tea towel, then allow to prove for approx. 2–2½ hours in a warm environment, approximately 26°C (78°F).

13. For baking, preheat the oven to 200°C (400°F), Gas Mark 6.

14. Eggwash your buns, then reduce the oven temperature down to 165°C (325°F), Gas Mark 3 and bake in the middle of the oven for 12–20 minutes. Let the buns cool before removing them from the tray.

Vanilla, Chocolate & Raspberry Babka

INGREDIENTS

DOUGH

210g	strong white bread flour, plus extra for dusting
85g	full-fat (whole) milk
50g	Sourdough Starter (optional, see pages 12–13)
45g	butter, softened, plus extra for greasing
40g	egg yolk
40g	sugar
10g	vegetable oil
5g	vanilla extract
4g	fast-action (active) dried yeast
3g	salt
5g	(unsweetened) cocoa powder

CHOCOLATE FILLING

160g	dark (semisweet) chocolate chips
pinch of salt	
40g	butter

STREUSEL

55g	strong white bread flour
50g	cold butter
100g	dark brown sugar
2g	(unsweetened) cocoa powder
1g	salt
raspberry jam – as needed	

METHOD

1. For the dough: in the bowl of a stand mixer fitted with a dough hook, combine all the ingredients except for the cocoa powder. Mix on slow speed until all the dry ingredients are absorbed and a dough forms, about 3–4 minutes.

2. Turn the mixer up to medium–high and mix until a smooth, strong dough forms, another 10–15 minutes.

3. Once the dough is strong, remove half of it from the mixer. With the other half of the dough in the stand mixer, add the cocoa powder and mix on slow speed until it is completely combined.

4. Place the chocolate dough on top of the vanilla dough in a bowl, cover with a tea towel and allow to prove in a warm area for 2 hours; it will almost double in size in that time.

5. In the meantime, prepare the chocolate filling and the streusel topping. For the chocolate filling, bring a small pot with 2.5cm (1 inch) of water to the boil. Place the chocolate chips, salt and butter in a metal bowl and place it on top of the pot of water.

6. Allow the chocolate and butter to melt completely, then whisk to combine. Reserve until ready to use.

(continued)

7. For the streusel, combine all the ingredients except the jam in a food processor. Run the food processor until everything is nicely combined, about 2 minutes. The mixture should compress together into chunks if you squeeze it. Reserve this mixture in the refrigerator until ready to use.

8. Once the dough has risen to about double in size, prepare a standard loaf tin (pan) by greasing it with soft butter.

9. Flour a work surface. Place the dough on the flour and sprinkle a little more flour on top.

10. With a rolling pin, roll the dough into a rectangle about 23cm (9 inches) wide and 30–35cm (12–14 inches) long; it should be about 5mm (¼ inch) thick.

11. Spread alternating strips of chocolate filling and raspberry jam horizontally across the dough, about 5cm (2 inches) per strip. You can use all chocolate filling or all raspberry jam, if you prefer.

12. Starting at the bottom edge of the dough, roll it into a spiral until you reach the far edge. You should end up with about a 23–25cm (9–10-inch) log. Using a knife, cut the log in half lengthways, so you have 2 pieces of dough that are about 25cm (10 inches) long.

13. Pick up one of the strips and turn it around, placing the whole edges of each dough together, with the exposed layer sides facing outward.

14. Pick up both pieces of dough at the same time and twist them together. Place them in the loaf tin (pan). Allow the dough to prove for another 1–2 hours, or until about doubled in size.

15. Meanwhile, preheat the oven to 180°C (350°C), Gas Mark 4.

16. Once the dough has risen, crumble the streusel over the top of the dough and bake for about 30–40 minutes, or until golden brown and baked to 93°C (199°F) internally.

17. Once baked, remove from the tin (pan) and allow to cool before enjoying.

Makes
6 PASTRIES

Walnut, Poppyseed & Plum Bostock

This recipe is ideal for using up slightly stale challah bread or brioche – in fact, it works better with bread that's a day or two old. I wanted to create something that echoes the flavours you'd find in desserts across Eastern Europe, including Ukraine – walnuts, poppyseeds, apple and cinnamon – and the frangipane is so delicious you could even make extra and freeze some for a future tart or galette!

INGREDIENTS

6   slices of day-old challah or brioche, about 2.5cm (1 inch) thick
3 large or 4 small plums, thinly sliced
demerara (turbinado) sugar or chopped walnuts, for decoration

FRANGIPANE

115g   unsalted butter, softened
100g   ground walnuts
pinch of sea salt flakes
½ tsp   ground cinnamon
85g   sugar
1   egg, at room temperature
½ tsp   vanilla extract
2 tbsp   plain (all-purpose) flour

SIMPLE SYRUP

150g   caster (superfine) sugar
½ tsp   ground cinnamon
150g   water

METHOD

1. Mix the butter, nuts, salt, cinnamon, sugar and egg together until combined, add the vanilla and flour and mix until just combined.

2. Cover and put in refrigerator for at least 1 hour and up to 24 hours. Take it out 15 minutes before you want to use it to make the Bostock so that it is easier to spread.

3. Preheat the oven to 160°C (325°F), Gas Mark 3, and line 2 baking trays (sheets) with nonstick baking paper.

4. Make the syrup: mix the sugar, cinnamon and water in a pan and bring to the boil. Cook for about 5 minutes on medium–low heat until the sugar has fully dissolved.

5. If your bread is fresh, pop it in the oven for a couple of minutes to dry out a bit so it will absorb the syrup better.

6. Dunk each slice quickly in the syrup on both sides, then place 3 slices on each lined baking tray (sheet).

7. Spread the frangipane all over the syrup-soaked bread, about 5mm (¼ inch) thick – not

too much or it will overflow, but you want enough to reach the edges so that it goes nice and toasty.

8. Put some slices of plum, fanned out, on top and sprinkle with demerara (turbinado) sugar or some chopped walnuts if you want a bit more crunch.

9. Bake for around 25 minutes until golden brown and toasty at the edges.

10. Let it cool for 1–2 minutes before you eat it as the fruit gets very hot – I like it served with some Greek yogurt or Skyr on the side. If you have leftover frangipane, it freezes well!

# CaKES

Helen Goh

**Makes
1 CAKE**

Blood Orange, Filo & Custard Cake

I love making this uncommonly delicious cake, a recipe from my friend Kathy Tsaples who owns a Greek deli in my home town, Melbourne. The method involves drying out filo (phyllo) pastry, then leaving it to soak in a custard made with yogurt, cream and the purée of a whole orange. After baking, the cake is doused in a fragrant cinnamon-infused syrup and left to sit, after which it develops a delightful texture, somewhere between a bread-and-butter pudding and a flourless orange cake. It is heavenly served with the yogurt honey cream.

INGREDIENTS

CAKE

300g	filo (phyllo) pastry
3	blood oranges
zest of 1 large lemon (save the juice for the syrup)	
3	eggs
150ml	oil
150g	caster (superfine) sugar
120g	Greek yogurt
120ml	pouring cream
½ tsp	vanilla extract
¾ tsp	baking powder
½ tsp	bicarbonate of soda (baking soda)
⅛ tsp	salt

SUGAR SYRUP

250g	caster (superfine) sugar
250g	water
4 tbsp	lemon juice (from 1 lemon)
juice of 1 large blood orange	
1	cinnamon stick
3	cloves

YOGURT CREAM

100g	Greek yogurt
100g	double (heavy) cream
½ tsp	vanilla extract
1 tbsp	runny honey
1 tbsp	icing (confectioners') sugar

METHOD

1. The day before baking the cake, unwrap the filo (phyllo) pastry and spread it out on a large baking tray (sheet) to dry out, uncovered, for 12–24 hours. Turn the pastry sheets over from time to time to make sure they dry evenly. Alternatively, spread out on 2 large baking trays (sheets) and bake at 100°C (210°F), Gas Mark ¼ for 10 minutes, then flip the pastry and bake for another 10 minutes.

2. Place 1 of the blood oranges in a small saucepan and cover with water. Place over a high heat and bring to the boil, then turn the heat down to medium-low and simmer

(continued)

for 1 hour. Remove the orange and allow it to cool, then slice into quarters, flicking out any seeds. Place in a food processor and process until it is a fine purée.

3. Add the lemon zest as well as the finely grated zest from 1 of the blood oranges (save the juice for the syrup), eggs, oil, sugar, yogurt, cream, vanilla, baking powder, bicarbonate of soda (baking soda) and salt. Pulse a few times to combine, then pour the mixture into a large mixing bowl.

4. Working in batches, tear or crumble the dried-out filo (phyllo) pastry into small pieces and add into the bowl with the yogurt and orange mix. Stir to prevent the sheets of filo (phyllo) from clumping together then leave to soak for about 30 minutes, stirring from time to time.

5. Meanwhile, prepare the sugar syrup for the cake: combine the sugar and water in a medium saucepan and bring to the boil. When the sugar has dissolved, add the lemon juice, blood orange juice (from the zested orange), cinnamon and cloves. Bring to the boil again, then turn the heat down to medium and simmer for 5 minutes. Set aside to cool, then strain into a jug.

6. Preheat the oven to 180°C (350°F), Gas Mark 4, then line the base and sides of a 20cm (8-inch) round cake tin (pan) with nonstick baking paper.

7. Cut the 1 remaining blood orange into 5mm- (¼-inch)-thick circles and arrange them on the bottom of the prepared cake tin.

8. Stir the soaked filo (phyllo) mixture, then carefully ladle it into the tin, directly over the orange slices.

9. Place in the oven and bake for 50–55 minutes or until a skewer inserted into the centre comes out clean. Remove from oven and immediately spoon the cooled syrup all over the top.

10. Allow the cake to absorb the syrup and cool completely before inverting on to a cake plate.

11. While the cake is cooling, make the yogurt cream by whisking all the ingredients by hand or using a cake mixer, until soft peaks form. Keep in the refrigerator until needed.

12. Serve the cake, sliced, with the yogurt cream on the side.

Jo Clarke & Aaron Kossoff
KOSSOFFS

Jewish Apple Cake

INGREDIENTS

APPLE

1	large Bramley apple, peeled, cored and ¾ chopped into 1.5cm (⅝ inch) chunks, ¼ thinly sliced
1 tbsp	caster (superfine) sugar,
1 tsp	ground cinnamon

CAKE

85g	vegetable oil
170g	caster (superfine) sugar
60g	orange juice
5g	vanilla extract
2	large eggs
180g	plain (all-purpose) flour
6g	salt
5g	baking powder
6g	ground cinnamon
honey, for drizzling	

METHOD

1. Preheat the oven to 170°C (335°F), Gas Mark 3. Grease an 18cm (7-inch) springform cake tin (pan) and line the bottom with nonstick baking paper.

2. Mix the apple slices with the caster (superfine) sugar and ground cinnamon. Stir to coat and leave to one side.

3. Put the vegetable oil, 170g caster (superfine) sugar, orange juice and vanilla extract into the bowl of a stand mixer fitted with a paddle attachment. Begin mixing at medium speed.

4. In a small bowl or jug, crack 1 of the eggs and then crack the other but reserve the white of the second egg.

5. Add the 1 egg and 1 egg yolk to the mixer, and mix until combined. Then add the chunks of apple to the mixer and mix on slow speed until the apple is incorporated.

6. Finally, add the flour, salt, baking powder and cinnamon to the mixer and continue mixing on slow speed until the batter is smooth.

7. Whisk the reserved egg white to soft peaks and then, very carefully, fold this into the batter using a spatula. Make sure it is totally incorporated and smooth.

(continued)

8. Slowly pour the batter into the cake tin. Finally, layer the thin slices of apple on top.

9. Bake in the middle shelf of the oven for 60–70 minutes or until a knife inserted into the middle comes out clean.

10. Remove from the oven and leave to cool slightly in the tin (pan) for 10 minutes. Then release the edges from the tin and drizzle honey over the top.

11. Cool and serve.

Drunken Eccles Cakes

Traditionally Eccles cakes are eaten with Lancashire cheese (as that's where they come from) but all and any cheese is good. Try them hot from the oven with a big slab of Cheddar in the middle. They feel like a winter treat or some part of a celebration, but I think you can eat them anytime at all. You can decide whether to soak the dried fruit in brandy or not, but it definitely gives them a nice kick. I have them for breakfast but that's because I really, *really* like them.

INGREDIENTS

CAKE

125g	unsalted butter, softened
125g	light brown sugar
2 tsp	ground cinnamon
1 tsp	garam masala
50g	dried mixed fruits, mixed with 1 tbsp brandy
500g	block of puff pastry, chilled

GLAZE

1	egg, beaten
1 tbsp	demerara (turbinado) sugar

METHOD

1. Line a baking tray (sheet) with nonstick baking paper.

2. With an electric whisk, or hands (my favourite utensil), combine the butter, sugar and spices, then gradually stir or scrunch in the brandy fruits. If it's very sticky, chill for 3–4 minutes.

3. Dampen your hands and roll your filling into small, golf-ball sized balls (roughly 30–40g). Place them on the lined tray (sheet) and pop them in the refrigerator.

4. Meanwhile, take the puff pastry from the refrigerator and roll it out until it's about 3mm (⅛ inch) thick.

5. With an 8cm (3¼-inch) cookie cutter, or rim of a big glass, cut out as many circles as you can, then pop a fruit ball on top of each one, like a bullseye.

6. Bring the edges together over the ball and pleat into the centre, pinching together to seal, then place seal-side down on the lined baking tray (sheet) and press down very slightly to

flatten the base of the ball and stabilize the Eccles cake —this stops it falling over in the oven.

7. Chill for 30 minutes.

8. Preheat the oven to 200°C (400°F), Gas Mark 6.

9. Brush over the beaten egg and sprinkle a pinch of demerara (turbinado) sugar on top of each Eccles cake.

10. With a sharp knife, cut 2 slits horizontally on top.

11. Bake for 20–25 minutes until crisp and golden. Let them sit for 5 minutes, then transfer to a wire rack to cool completely. These are very good with a hunk of cheese on the side.

Mette Marie Sarbo & Kathrine Rosamunde
H.U.G BAGERI

Makes
1 CAKE OR 10 MUFFINS

Gluten-Free Lemon & Almond Cake

INGREDIENTS

CAKE

200g	butter (or dairy-free alternative), softened
200g	cane sugar (coconut sugar is also lovely, but will give a darker cake)
4	eggs
200g	almond flour
80g	gluten-free flour (like rice or sorghum)
1 tsp	baking powder
1 tsp	vanilla extract

zest of 2 organic lemons or bergamots

ICING (FROSTING)

150g   icing (confectioners') sugar
pinch of ground turmeric, for colour
4 tbsp   lemon juice (from 1 lemon)
dried flowers and chopped pistachios, to decorate (optional)

METHOD

1. Preheat the oven to 170°C (335°F), Gas Mark 3.

2. Beat the butter and sugar well together.

3. Beat in 1 egg at a time, then add the rest of the ingredients and whisk it all together.

4. Bake in a 24cm round, springform tin (pan), or loaf tin (pan), for about 35–40 minutes. Check with a toothpick to see if the middle is set.

5. Make the icing (frosting) by stirring the icing (confectioner's) sugar and turmeric into the lemon juice until you have a smooth consistency.

6. Let the cake cool and cover it with the icing (frosting). You can decorate with dried flowers and chopped pistachios.

7. This is also great baked as muffins; the mixture will yield about 10–12 pieces. Bake them for about 20 minutes!

Angharad Conway & Lance Gardner
TY MELIN BAKERY

Makes
16 PORTIONS

Apple & Soured Cream Cake

This recipe is perfect for all seasons, you can substitute the apple for any fruits that are in season throughout the year. Peach and raspberry, blueberry, apricot, plum are all delicious substitutes.

INGREDIENTS

TOPPING

425g	butter, diced
375g	light brown sugar
280g	plain (all-purpose) flour
375g	jumbo oats
2 tsp	bicarbonate of soda (baking soda)
2 tsp	ground cinnamon
1 tsp	mixed (apple pie) spice

FILLING

375g	soured cream
200g	caster (superfine) sugar
35g	plain (all-purpose) flour
2	eggs
500g	grated apple

METHOD

1. Preheat the oven to 170°C (335°F), Gas Mark 3. Line a 20 x 30cm (8 x 12 inches) rectangle baking tin (pan) with nonstick baking paper.

2. Get out the ingredients for the topping. In a stand mixer fitted with the paddle attachment, cream the butter and sugar for 3 minutes on high speed. Scrape down the mixing bowl with a spatula and then mix again on high speed for 2 minutes.

3. Add all the rest of the topping ingredients and mix on slow speed for 2 minutes. Press 600g of the topping into the lined baking tin (pan); use wet hands for help getting into the corners. Place the remaining crumble mixture in the fridge, ready for use later in the recipe.

4. Bake for 30–40 minutes till golden brown.

5. Mix the filling ingredients together in a bowl and whisk.

6. When the base is baked add the filling and add the remainder of the crumble topping. It's okay if you see some of the cream while adding the topping.

7. Bake again at 170°C (335°F), Gas Mark 3 for 30–40 minutes till golden brown and set to touch and then leave to cool.

Alice Mohan
ALICE

Makes
15–18 PIECES

Brunsviger

INGREDIENTS

DOUGH

325g	cold water
325g	full-fat (whole) milk, cold
130g	sugar
22g	salt
30g	fresh yeast
1.25kg	strong white bread flour
75g	butter, softened

FILLING

550g	dark brown sugar
400g	butter
15g	freshly ground espresso beans
6g	salt
100g	candied orange peel

TOPPING

orange zest

METHOD

1. Add all the dough ingredients to the bowl of a stand mixer fitted with a dough hook and knead for 10–12 minutes.

2. Let the dough rest for 15 minutes.

3. Roll the dough into a flat rectangular shape that will fit the baking tray (sheet) that the brunsviger is going to be baked in. I use one that's about 30 × 40cm (12 × 16 inches).

4. Place nonstick baking paper at the bottom of the baking tray (sheet) and place the dough on top. Let the dough rest and prove for about 90 minutes or until at least doubled in size.

5. Preheat the oven to 180°C (350°C), Gas Mark 4.

6. Now make the filling: add all the filling ingredients to a thick-bottomed pot over a medium heat and melt and stir until homogeneous. Allow to cool.

7. When the dough is ready and doubled in size, make little holes in the dough with wet hands, just as if you were making focaccia.

8. Pour the filling on to the dough and make sure it is evenly distributed. Bake immediately in the middle of the oven for about 22–25 minutes.

9. Allow the brunsviger to rest for about 30 minutes to 1 hour before cutting into squares. Finish with freshly grated orange zest.

Makes
1 CAKE

Buckwheat & Honey Cake

I've always felt this cake is full of good wishes. At Friends & Family we make it during the first few weeks of autumn, when many of our customers celebrate Rosh Hashanah, the arrival of the Jewish new year. Rich with dark and full-flavoured buckwheat honey, it represents new beginnings as much as it exemplifies the symbiotic relationship between the bees and the buckwheat flowers they pollinate in order to collect the flowers' pollen and make their precious honey.

INGREDIENTS

105g	plain (all-purpose) flour
110g	buckwheat flour
¾ tsp	bicarbonate of soda (baking soda)
1 tsp	ground cinnamon
1 tsp	kosher (flaky) salt
150g	caster (superfine) sugar
2	large eggs
300ml	vegetable oil
180ml	apple sauce
120ml	buckwheat honey, plus 2 tbsp for glazing the top

METHOD

1. Preheat the oven to 150°C (300°F), Gas Mark 2. Lightly coat the bottom and sides of a 23cm (9-inch) round springform cake tin (pan) with nonstick spray.

2. Sift the flours, bicarb (baking soda), cinnamon and salt into a medium bowl. In a separate bowl, whisk together the sugar, eggs, vegetable oil, apple sauce and 120ml honey.

3. Make a well in the centre of the dry ingredients with your hands. Pour the liquid mixture into the well and whisk to combine.

4. Pour the batter into the prepared tin (pan). Place on the middle shelf of the oven and bake for 30 minutes.

5. Rotate the cake and bake for another 20–25 minutes, until a toothpick inserted in the centre comes out clean. Rotating the tin halfway through the baking process will ensure that the cake bakes evenly.

(continued)

6. Remove from the oven and set aside to cool for 1 hour.

7. To unmould, run an offset spatula or paring knife along the side of the tin (pan) and loosen the springform lock. Transfer to a cake plate.

8. Warm the 2 tablespoons honey in a small sauté pan (or in the microwave) for about 1 minute and brush this over the top of the cake. The cake will keep for a couple of days in an airtight container at room temperature. It can also be frozen for up to 2 weeks – just make sure to wrap tightly with plastic to avoid freezer burn.

NOTES & VARIATION

While not necessarily a traditional Jewish recipe, this cake made with fresh milled buckwheat flour and buckwheat honey leaves you wanting nothing more. The cake calls for a generous helping of apple sauce, which is commonly used in baked goods more typical of this holiday. In spite of the symbolism of its origins and complexity of its flavours, this cake is very easy to prepare. The resulting cake is moist and aromatic, with hints of perfumed honey and cinnamon, and has the robust colour of buckwheat. I like to brush the baked cake with a thin coat of additional buckwheat honey for a luscious appeal.

As the winter holidays approach, you might feel compelled to prepare the variation below that uses rye flour instead of buckwheat, and a smidge of warm spices. Regardless of which flour you use, do pay attention to the oven temperature; due to the recipe's high honey content, it must be baked at 150°C (300°F), Gas Mark 2, to prevent a burned honey aftertaste.

RYE HONEY CAKE: For a sober and elegant version, evocative of the traditional French spiced cake known as *pain d'épices*, substitute 125g dark rye flour for the buckwheat flour and supplement the cinnamon with the following spices: ½ teaspoon ground cloves, ½ teaspoon ground cardamom, ½ teaspoon freshly grated nutmeg and ½ teaspoon ground ginger.

Ixta Belfrage

Cassava, Coconut & Passion Fruit Cake

My Brazilian mother loves the combination of cassava (or *macaxeira*, as we know it), coconut and passion fruit and asks for this cake every year on her birthday. I adore its unique texture; it's caramelized and crispy on the outside and chewy and springy on the inside, sort of like mochi, if you've tried that. It isn't overly sweet, which makes it the perfect mid-morning or afternoon treat with a cup of coffee.

INGREDIENTS

1kg	cassava root (or 500g shop-bought frozen grated cassava, defrosted)
8	passion fruits
100g	unsalted butter, plus extra for greasing
100g	caster (superfine) sugar, plus 2½ tbsp for coating and sprinkling
140g	canned coconut milk (at least 70% coconut extract)
100g	condensed milk
50g	desiccated coconut
1	egg, whisked
2 tsp	tangerine or orange zest (from 2 tangerines)
1½ tsp	lime zest (from 2 limes)
1 tsp	vanilla bean paste
⅛ tsp	fine salt
sea salt flakes	

METHOD

1. Preheat the oven to 200°C (400°F), Gas Mark 6.

2. Peel the cassava roots, removing the thick brown skin as well as the pinkish layer beneath it. Don't use any part of the cassava that's black or soft.

3. Finely grate the cassava using the smaller holes of a box grater – you should get 600g. Transfer the grated cassava to a colander and place in the sink.

4. Squeeze the grated cassava vigorously to get rid of as much liquid as possible; you should end up with 500g squeezed cassava. Transfer to a large bowl and set aside.

5. Halve the passion fruits and scoop the flesh into a sieve set over the bowl of grated cassava. Push down on the flesh with a spoon to extract all the liquid. Discard the seeds.

6. Grease a 20cm (8-inch) nonstick cake tin (pan) with butter – make sure the tin is completely covered in butter.

(continued)

7. Add 1½ tablespoons of the sugar to the tin and shake to ensure the buttery sides and bottom are completely covered with the sugar.

8. Melt the 100g butter in a pan over a low heat until beginning to brown and smell caramelized, about 6 minutes. Cool for a few minutes.

9. Add the browned butter, 100g sugar, coconut milk, condensed milk, desiccated coconut, egg, tangerine or orange zest, lime zest, vanilla bean pasta and fine salt to the bowl with the grated cassava. Mix until thoroughly combined.

10. Spoon into the cake tin (pan), level the surface, then sprinkle the remaining 1 tablespoon of sugar evenly over to cover.

11. Bake for 50–55 minutes until the top is crisp and golden brown, rotating the tin (pan) halfway so the cake colours evenly. Leave to cool for 5 minutes, then run a knife around the edge of the cake to release it from the tin.

12. Place a rack over the tin (pan), then flip the cake out on to the rack. The cake should end up on the plate but if not, carefully release it from the bottom (or top once flipped) of the tin with a knife or spatula.

13. Leave to cool and set for at least 30 minutes (this is very important!) then sprinkle with flaked salt.

14. Use a sharp serrated knife to slice and enjoy with coffee.

NOTES

The only time-consuming part of this recipe is peeling, grating and squeezing the cassava, after which all the ingredients come together very simply in a bowl. I tend to use frozen grated cassava (available online and in many East Asian supermarkets) which makes the process a lot quicker.

Makes
8 TEACAKES

Currant Teacakes

Teacakes have always been a fond favourite of mine and something that reminds me of my childhood in the best possible way. Here at Marmadukes they have been really quite popular, and it brings me joy every day to be able to make them for the people of Sheffield. I find the best way to enjoy them is toasted and with lashings of butter.

INGREDIENTS

SPONGE

150g	T65 (French white bread) flour (I use wild-farmed but any white bread flour will be fine)
100g	water
1g	fresh yeast

FRUIT SOAKER

100g	brewed Earl Grey tea
200g	dried currants
zest of 1 orange	
zest of 1 lemon	

MAIN DOUGH

350g	T65 (French white bread) flour, plus extra for dusting
200g	water
3g	fresh yeast
8g	salt
20g	milk powder
60g	butter
40g	honey

METHOD

1. Prepare sponge the day before baking. This is done by adding the yeast to the water and then mixing by hand with the flour. Once mixed cover and leave out at room temperature overnight.

2. Also the day before, add your currants and the orange and lemon zests to the Earl Grey tea. Leave this in a container overnight to allow the currants to soak up the tea and become plump and juicy.

3. The following day, mix the dough including the sponge prepared the day before by adding all the ingredients apart from the butter, honey and fruit soaker to the bowl of a stand mixer. Mix with a dough hook at a slow speed for 8-10 minutes until the dough is smooth and almost developed.

4. Add the butter and honey and mix at a fast speed (but not full speed) for 3–5 minutes to allow the dough to fully develop. The dough should look nice and smooth.

5. Finally add the soaker and mix on a slow speed to combine the currants well. This should only take a few minutes.

6. Remove the bowl from the mixer, cover and leave the dough to ferment until it has doubled in size, roughly 1–2 hours at 22°C (71.5°F).

7. Once the dough has doubled in size, gently tip the dough on to a well-floured work surface and cut into 8 even portions weighing 150g each. Gently pre-shape into round balls.

8. Once shaped, allow to rest for 10 minutes.

9. Line a baking tray (sheet). Round off the dough again, place on the lined tray and flatten slightly with the palm of your hand.

10. Cover and allow to prove at 30°C (86°F) for a further 45 minutes or until the dough balls have doubled in size.

11. Preheat the oven to 230°C (450°F), Gas Mark 8.

12. Before putting in the oven, brush the tops of the teacakes with water. Bake for 12–15 minutes until golden brown on top.

David Gingell
BIG JO

Makes
20

Rum Babas

INGREDIENTS

RUM BABAS

250g	T80 (strong) flour, plus extra for dusting
	handful of chopped, soaked raisins
	pinch of salt
10g	sugar
7g	fresh yeast
15g	water, at hand temperature
4	eggs
12g	butter, melted, plus extra for greasing
	handful of chopped, soaked raisins, plus extra to serve

SYRUP

1.2kg	caster (superfine) sugar
2 litres	water
	zest of 1 orange
½	vanilla pod (bean)
350ml	dark rum, plus extra to serve

VANILLA CREAM

250ml	double (heavy) cream
½	vanilla pod (bean)
25g	caster (superfine) sugar

apricot jam

METHOD

1. Put the flour, salt and sugar in the bowl of a stand mixer fitted with a dough hook. Dissolve the yeast in the water. Incorporate the eggs and water into the flour, mix until smooth and glossy, for approx. 15 minutes.

2. Cover with a tea towel and prove the mix for around 1½ hours or doubled in size.

3. Knock back the mix and add the melted butter in 3 parts, beating with the dough hook until incorporated. Mix in the soaked raisins.

4. Coat the insides of 20 baba moulds with butter and flour. Transfer the dough to a piping (pastry) bag and pipe the dough into the bottom of each mould to around halfway up the mould. Prove again until the dough is rising out the top of the moulds with a nice dome shape.

5. Preheat the oven to 185°C (365°F), Gas Mark 4, then bake for 15 minutes.

6. Bring all the syrup ingredients except the rum to a boil in a pan and then take off the heat to cool. Once cool, add the dark rum. Dip the babas in the warm syrup until they are saturated. Remove and let then drain on a rack.

7. In a bowl, lightly whip all of the vanilla cream ingredients together.

8. To serve brush, with a little with apricot jam and a shot of rum. Serve with a healthy dollop of vanilla cream and extra raisins.

Ginger & Rye Loaf Cake

INGREDIENTS

90g	plain (all-purpose) flour
60g	dark rye flour
¼ tsp	cinnamon
¼ tsp	salt
65g	fresh root ginger, peeled and sliced into coins
100g	caster (superfine) sugar
115g	grapeseed oil, plus extra for greasing
130g	black treacle
130g	boiling water (see recipe)
1 tsp	bicarbonate of soda (baking soda)
1	egg

METHOD

1. Preheat the oven to 120°C (250°F), Gas Mark ½. Brush a loaf tin (pan) with oil and line the bottom with nonstick baking paper.

2. Sift the plain (all-purpose) flour, rye flour, cinnamon and salt into a large bowl. Set aside.

3. Place the ginger and sugar in a blender and whiz until the ginger begins to release its juices and forms a smooth paste. Stop the machine and scrape down the sides to make sure all of the ginger is incorporated.

4. Feel free to drizzle some of the oil into the blender to keep things moving. Once the mixture is smooth and there are no more bits of ginger, add the rest of the oil. Turn off the blender and add the treacle.

5. Bring a pot of water to a rolling boil. Quickly but carefully measure 130g of the water, then discard the rest. Place the measured water back into the pot and return it to the heat.

6. Keeping close watch, bring it to another rolling boil, then add the bicarbonate of soda (baking soda). Immediately remove from the heat and, with the blender off, pour into the ginger mixture.

(continued)

7. Use a spatula to gently stir the mixture (this will help to loosen the treacle.) Carefully pulse the blender a few times until all the wet ingredients are fully incorporated.

8. Place the bowl of flour over a damp towel to secure it, then create a well in the middle of the flour.

9. With the blender jug in one hand and a whisk in the other, slowly add the wet ingredients into the dry, whisking to incorporate. Take care to avoid any lumps of flour, and whisk just enough to incorporate everything.

10. Scrape the bottom and sides of the bowl with a spatula, then finally whisk in the egg until everything is smooth.

11. Pour into your prepared loaf tin (pan) and place on to a rack in the middle of the oven.

12. Bake for 30 minutes, then rotate and bake for another 15 minutes.

13. Turn the oven up to 150°C (300°F), Gas Mark 2, and continue to cook until set (another 5–10 minutes).

14. In summer, serve with strawberries, blackberries, peaches or plums and whipped cream. It is also delicious with pears or roasted quince in autumn, or warm poached prunes in winter.

Lily Jones
LILY VANILLI

Makes
1 CAKE

Sticky Coconut Cake

This is my favourite sticky, fluffy coconut cake, which we make and serve in the bakery all summer. It's quick, really simple and lasts like a dream for about a week if you wrap it airtight. This can be scaled up or down and made as cupcakes or layer cakes. It can be iced as you like but I've included notes on how I do mine.

INGREDIENTS

COCONUT CAKE

170g	unsalted butter, softened, plus extra for greasing
300g	caster (superfine) sugar
3	eggs
240g	plain (all-purpose) flour
2½ tsp	baking powder
1 tsp	fine salt
200ml	full-fat coconut milk
35g	desiccated coconut (plus extra for decoration)

SWISS MERINGUE

150g	egg white
200g	caster (superfine) sugar
400g	unsalted butter, softened

BUTTERCREAM

100g	unsalted butter, softened
300g	golden icing (confectioners') sugar, sifted
1 tsp	vanilla extract
75ml	double (heavy) crea

METHOD

COCONUT CAKE

1. Preheat the oven to 180°C (350°C), Gas Mark 4. Grease 2 18cm (7-inch) cake tins (pans).

2. In the bowl of a stand mixer, cream together the soft butter and sugar until light and fluffy – about 3 minutes or until it looks much lighter and aerated.

3. Now add the eggs and mix on slow, until just combined evenly into the batter.

4. In another bowl, mix together the flour, baking powder and salt, then add this to the batter and mix just to evenly incorporate.

5. Add the coconut milk and desiccated coconut and mix to just incorporate; there's no need to beat this much, just enough to combine evenly so you have a nice smooth batter.

6. Now divide evenly between the 2 greased cake tins (pans) and bake in the oven for 20 minutes. Check if they are done (they probably need a little longer) – they're ready

(continued)

when a toothpick inserted in the centre comes out clean.

7. When they are done, carefully turn the cakes out on to a cooling rack.

8. While your cakes are cooling, toast the coconut in the oven at 180°C (350°C), Gas Mark 4. for around 6 minutes – stirring occasionally – until it's aromatic and a nice even golden brown.

SWISS MERINGUE

1. Bring a large pan of water to the boil. Place the egg whites and sugar in a large heatproof bowl over (but not touching) the simmering water and cook the egg whites and sugar for around 5 minutes. Stir the egg and sugar occasionally, to ensure it doesn't start to cook

2. It's done when you can't feel any sugar crystals when you rub some mix between thumb and finger. Then beat the whites until stiff.

3. Then add the butter; the time it takes to come together into a smooth buttercream can really vary depending on exactly how soft your butter is, mine took around 3 minutes here but can take twice that – just keep going till it's done.

BUTTERCREAM

1. Beat the butter in the bowl of a stand mixer for 4–5 minutes on high speed. Then add the sugar, vanilla and cream and beat on a low speed to bring it together. Turn up the speed and beat on high for another 2–3 minutes.

TO FINISH THE CAKE

1. To make the icing (frosting), use an approx. 50/50 mix of the Swiss meringue and buttercream. Just mix them together evenly by hand or with the paddle attachment on your stand mixer.

2. When the cakes have completely cooled, sandwich them together with your icing (frosting) and spread more on top – you can just use a spoon for this, or a palette knife (frosting spatula) but I think it looks best when it's rough, so don't stress over this part! Then top with the toasted desiccated coconut.

Cannelés

Cannelés are those gorgeous little honey-infused baked treats, traditionally served in the morning and originating from Bordeaux in France. They are now found in cool cafés and awesome bakeries all over the world and I absolutely love them. A real feature of these pastries is the beeswax used to line the cannelé moulds and the perfume and crunch it gives the finished product. Google local apiaries or seek a community urban bee company and ask them if you can purchase beeswax. They always have lots left over from honey harvest so it's not an uncommon thing to ask for these days.

INGREDIENTS

500ml	full-fat (whole) milk
I	vanilla pod (bean), seeds scraped
50g	unsalted butter
2	eggs, lightly beaten
2	egg yolks, lightly beaten
150g	icing (confectioners') sugar, sifted
125g	plain (all-purpose) flour
100g	honey
	capful of rum
	zest of I orange

BEESWAX MOULDS

| 75g | beeswax |
| 75g | butter, clarified |

METHOD

1. Bring the milk and vanilla seeds just to a boil in a saucepan. Set aside and keep warm.

2. Melt the butter in a small saucepan over a low–medium heat to 'nut butter' stage. It will bubble up, froth and start to turn to a golden-brown colour; it is ready at this point, and you will smell an amazing nutty perfume.

3. Pour the butter straight into the pot of warm milk and set aside.

4. Mix the eggs and egg yolks together in a small bowl.

5. Sift the icing (confectioners') sugar and flour into a mixing bowl. Add the eggs and stir gently with a fork.

(continued)

6. Pour the warm liquid into the bowl and further mix with the fork or a spatula to eradicate lumps. Try not to beat too much air into the batter at this stage.

7. Stir in the honey, rum and zest. Transfer this mixture to a container and store in the refrigerator for a minimum of 24 hours.

8. After 24 hours, remove the batter from the refrigerator and strain it through a sieve into a jug or container. Store in the refrigerator or use immediately.

9. Preheat the oven to 200°C (400°F), Gas Mark 6.

10. Gently stir the batter with a spoon to unsettle the flour, which may have settled to the bottom of the container.

11. Pour the batter ¾ of the way up each of 24 prepared cannelé moulds (see right) and place the moulds on a baking tray (sheet).

12. Put the tray (sheet) in the oven and bake the cannelés for 30 minutes before turning the tray around and cooking them for a further 15 minutes until dark brown.

13. Remove from the oven and leave them to cool for 10 minutes in the mould; this ensures the crispy exterior. Set a timer for this as if you leave them too long to cool in the mould you run the risk of them sticking.

14. Turn the cannelés out after the 10 minutes and leave to cool on cooling rack. Consume on the day.

BEESWAX MOULDS

1. Prepare your cannelé moulds by warming them for 10 minutes in an oven preheated to 150°C (300°F), Gas Mark 2.

2. Gently melt the beeswax in a small saucepan over a low heat.

3. Add the clarified butter and mix to combine. Reheat the mix and pour into a warmed cannelé mould up to the lip. Use tongs or an oven glove or cloth to pour the mixture back into the saucepan, thus lining the mould.

4. Turn the mould upside down on a rack placed over a baking tray (sheet). Repeat with each mould and finally put the rack and tray into the oven to heat for 5 minutes.

5. Remove the rack and tray from the oven and leave to cool. Any beeswax mix that drips on to the tray can be scraped into the saucepan and used again. Please be careful not to pour any excess beeswax down the drain as it WILL block your sink.

Coffee, Cardamom & Walnut Cake

Coffee and walnut is a classic British combo, and one of our favourite cakes – the kind you have in the café at a Tate gallery or a National Trust property. Coffee with cardamom is a Middle Eastern staple. It made sense to me that the three flavours would work well together, and they do. Even though the spice adds a tiny exotic note, this cake could take pride of place in any cafeteria across the land.

INGREDIENTS

butter, for greasing
330g   icing (confectioners') sugar
120g   ground almonds
130g   self-raising flour
pinch of table salt
80g   walnuts, roasted, plus 50g to garnish
1 tsp   ground coffee (Turkish coffee powder is best)
½ tsp   ground cardamom
3   eggs
150g   egg whites (about 4 eggs)
140g   burned butter (see note overleaf)

SYRUP

2 tbsp honey
60ml   water
50g   caster (superfine) sugar
double espresso or 60ml strong coffee

ICING (FROSTING)

120g   unsalted butter, at room temperature
140g   icing (confectioners') sugar
400g   full-fat cream cheese, at room temperature
30g   date molasses or maple syrup
1 tsp   ground coffee (Turkish coffee powder is best)

METHOD

1. Preheat the oven to 190°C (375°F), Gas Mark 5. Butter a 23cm (9-inch) cake tin (pan) and line with nonstick baking paper.

2. Stir the dry ingredients together in a large bowl, then add the eggs and egg whites and mix really well until smooth.

3. Pour in the warm melted butter and stir carefully until fully combined. Transfer to the prepared tin (pan) and allow to sit for 10 minutes to rest the batter a little, then bake for about 30–35 minutes until the cake is set.

4. While the cake is baking, bring the syrup ingredients to the boil in a pan, then remove from the heat.

5. Once the cake comes out of the oven, brush it generously with half the syrup, reserving the remainder for later. Chill the cake (still in its tin) in the refrigerator for at least 1 hour (and up to 24 hours).

6. Put the butter and icing (confectioners') sugar in the bowl of a stand a mixer fitted

(continued)

with a paddle attachment and cream together on a high speed until really light and fluffy.

7. Mix in the cream cheese a little at a time, allowing each addition to combine and aerate before adding the next.

8. Finally mix in the date molasses or maple syrup together with the ground coffee. Scrape the sides and bottom of the bowl to check the icing (frosting) is well combined with no lumps.

9. Remove the cake from the tin (pan), place on a serving platter and use a large, serrated knife to cut it in half to create 2 layers. This can seem a little scary, but it is just a question of confidence. Use the knife to score around the sides of the cake at the midline to give you a guideline to follow. Holding the knife firmly in one hand, place the other hand flat on the top of the cake (to keep it steady) and use little sawing motions to cut through it, all the way to the other side.

10. Very gently slide the top layer on to your work surface or a flat baking tray (sheet). Brush the cut surface of the bottom layer with the remaining syrup, then cover with half the icing (frosting), spreading it all over, right up to the edges.

11. Very carefully lift up the top layer of cake and slide it to sit on the iced bottom layer. Spread the rest of the icing (frosting) over the top in little waves and garnish with walnuts.

12. You will need to keep this cake in the refrigerator. It will be tasty for 2–3 days, but make sure to bring it back up to room temperature before eating for the best result.

NOTES

Burned butter, or beurre noisette as it is called in French, is made by heating butter in a saucepan until the water boils off and the milk particles turn a dark golden colour and develop a lovely nutty flavour.

Makes
I CAKE

Ricotta, Olive Oil & Lemon Cake

This cake is everything you want from an olive oil cake: damp and rich. This recipe is designed to really celebrate the texture of the ricotta and the heady flavour of the olive. Use an oil that is bright and fruity. This cake will take really well to any fruity addition. I've added plenty of lemon zest in this case but stone fruits, grapes or even herbs like wild fennel or rosemary would be delicious here, too. Simply fold your chosen fruit or herb through the batter at the end.

INGREDIENTS

275ml	olive oil, plus extra for greasing
4	eggs
200g	caster (superfine) sugar
250g	ricotta
150g	ground almonds
100g	polenta
2 tsp	baking powder
I tsp	fine salt
zest of 4 lemons	
2 tbsp	demerara (turbinado) sugar
4 tbsp	lemon juice (from I lemon)

METHOD

1. Preheat the oven to 170°C (335°F), Gas Mark 3. Line a 23cm (9-inch) springform tin (pan) with nonstick baking paper on the base and grease with a little oil on the sides.

2. In a large bowl, whisk the olive oil and eggs together. You don't need to create volume, just
to make sure they are all well homogenized.

3. In a separate bowl, beat the caster (superfine) sugar and ricotta together until smooth and then add to the eggs and oil.

4. Finally add the ground almonds, polenta, baking powder, salt and lemon zest and mix well.

5. Pour the batter into the prepared tin (pan) and sprinkle it with demerara (turbinado) sugar on top.

6. Bake in the oven for 50 minutes to 1 hour. As soon as the cake is ready and comes out of the oven, pour over the lemon juice. Allow to cool and serve.

Gluten-Free Chocolate & Tonka Cakes

INGREDIENTS

WHIPPING CHOCOLATE GANACHE

300ml	double (heavy) cream
75g	dark (semisweet) chocolate (72% cocoa solids)
75g	milk chocolate (33% cocoa solids)

CHOCOLATE CAKE

250g	unsalted butter
200g	ground almonds
50g	unsweetened cocoa powder
75g	rice flour
375g	icing (confectioners') sugar
300g	egg white (about 10 eggs)

½ piece of tonka bean, to decorate

METHOD

1. The day before you bake your cupcakes, bring the cream to the boil in a small saucepan.

2. Place both the chocolates in a large heatproof mixing bowl, then pour the cream over the chocolate. Wait a couple of minutes and then, with a hand blender, mix until it is completely smooth. Place in a container and leave overnight in the refrigerator.

3. Preheat the oven to 160°C (325°F), Gas Mark 3 and place a muffin silicone mould on a baking tray (sheet).

4. In a saucepan, gently heat the butter until the colour starts to become nutty brown, then remove from the heat to slightly cool.

5. Place the remaining chocolate cake ingredients in a large mixing bowl. Slowly pour the brown butter into the bowl and mix, then fill each silicone muffin hole almost to the top.

6. Bake in the oven for 25–35 minutes. To see if they are cooked, gently place a cake skewer in one of the cakes: if it comes back clean, your cake is ready. If not, simply place it back in the oven until it is cooked. Once cooked, remove from the oven and leave to cool completely.

7. Whisk the ganache until it looks like whipped cream. Transfer into a piping (pastry) bag and pipe on top of the cooled cakes, then top with grated tonka bean.

Kugelhopf

Kugelhopf is very popular from my hometown in Alsace (region of France). It's has been a big part of my apprenticeship of being a baker in France and has a special place in my heart, from my origins and where I grew up. It's a rich sweet bread we love to share with family and friends on a weekend and breakfast. The topping ingredients could be different to the recipe I'm sharing. You could include some nuts such as pecans or walnuts, or other fruit.... You could even make it savoury with the right ingredients. So what's not to like about these?!

INGREDIENTS

MACERATION

75g	dried orange and lemon, chopped
75g	sultanas (golden raisins)
zest of ½ orange	
zest of ½ lemon	
I	vanilla pod (bean)
200g	water

DOUGH

500g	T55 (French white bread) flour
150g	eggs (shelled weight)
150g	full-fat (whole) milk
75g	caster (superfine) sugar
15g	fast-action (active) dried yeast
10g	salt
175g	unsalted butter, at around 10°C (50°F), plus extra for greasing
12	whole almonds, for the mould
icing (confectioners') sugar, for decoration (optional)	

METHOD

1. Soak the fruit for the maceration together in a bowl for 24 hours.

2. In the bowl of a stand mixer fitted with a dough hook, mix all the dough ingredients except the butter and almonds on slow speed for 5 minutes and then on fast speed for 6–8 minutes.

3. Add the butter and mix it on slow speed until fully incorporated.

4. Finish by adding the macerated ingredients into the mixer on slow speed until well incorporated.

5. Transfer the dough to a large mixing bowl and leave to rise for 3 hours with a stretch and fold halfway through (see page 66, step 4); this is best done at ambient temperature room (around 23°C/73.5°F).

6. Divide the dough into 3 portions of 450g, then shape into balls. Leave it rest in the refrigerator for 30 minutes to relax.

7. Prepare your Kugelhopf moulds by melting the extra butter for greasing and brushing the inside of the mould with it. Arrange the whole almonds on the bottom of the tin.

8. Remove your dough from the refrigerator and shape it into a round. Make a hole in the middle and press the nice and smooth part of the dough into the almonds.

9. Cover with a tea towel and let it prove for around 2½ hours.

10. Preheat the oven to 170°C (335°F), Gas Mark 3, then bake the dough for 40 minutes.

11. Once cooked, remove from the moulds and check if the Kugelhopf is well baked. It should be golden brown and well risen and a skewer inserted into the middle of the cake should come out clean. Cool on a wire rack.

12. As a decoration you can use some icing (confectioners') sugar.

NOTES

Put all the dough ingredients in the refrigerator the day before so that they are cold. While mixing, be sure to not allow the dough to get too warm. Return to the fridge to re-chill if needed.

The baking time and temperature set up could differ depending on the oven you are using, so keep a little eye on it.

COOKIES / BISCUITS

Michael James

Anzac Biscuits

I use wholemeal flour for more flavour and wholesomeness. For variation, I also like to add 100g of currants in with the wet ingredients, just before adding the bicarbonate of soda (baking soda). Of course, then it can no longer be called an Anzac biscuit (cookie). When mixing this dough, it is handy to cover your hands with a little oil or water to stop it from sticking to your fingers and make it easier to work with. When measuring the golden syrup (or corn syrup), coat the spoon with a little mild-flavoured vegetable oil to get an accurate measurement and avoid a sticky mess. You can freeze these biscuits to bake later, in which case you will need to let them defrost first.

INGREDIENTS

200g	soft light brown sugar
150g	wholemeal flour
120g	rolled oats
50g	desiccated coconut
125g	butter
50g	golden syrup (or corn syrup)
20g	water
½ tsp	bicarbonate of soda (baking soda)

METHOD

1. Preheat the oven to 160°C (325°C), Gas Mark 3. Line 2 baking trays (sheets) with nonstick baking paper.

2. Put the sugar, flour, oats and coconut in a medium bowl, and mix to combine.

3. Put the butter, golden syrup (or corn syrup) and water in a medium saucepan over a low heat, and stir until the butter has melted and the mixture is nice and syrupy.

4. Add the bicarbonate of soda (baking soda) and mix well. The mixture will fizz up a little on reacting with the soda.

5. Pour the syrup over the dry ingredients and mix with your hands until well combined.

(continued)

6. Divide the dough into 12 even balls. Gently flatten each ball with the palm of your hand until you have 2cm- (¾ inch)-high discs.

7. Space out the biscuits evenly on the lined trays (sheets) – they will expand a little during baking so make sure you leave enough space around each one.

8. Bake for 10 minutes, turn the trays and bake for another 5 minutes until lightly golden brown. I like my biscuits a little chewy, but if you prefer a crispier finish, leave them in the oven for another couple of minutes.

9. Place the biscuits on a wire rack to cool. Store at room temperature in an airtight container.

Ben Lines
GWYN'S BAKERY

Chocolate & Ginger Cookies

INGREDIENTS

125g	vegetable oil
175g	dark brown sugar
105g	caster (superfine) sugar
65g	oat milk
235g	wholemeal flour
3g	bicarbonate of soda (baking soda)
3g	baking powder
3g	salt
9g	ground ginger
95g	stem ginger, finely chopped
95g	vegan milk chocolate chips

METHOD

1. In a large mixing bowl, add the vegetable oil, dark brown sugar, caster (superfine) sugar and oat milk and whisk together until well combined.

2. Then add the flour, bicarbonate of soda (baking soda), baking powder and salt. Stir with a spatula until smooth.

3. Then add the ground ginger, finely chopped stem ginger, and chocolate chips and mix until evenly incorporated.

4. Place the dough in the refrigerator and chill for 1 hour.

5. Preheat the oven to 160°C (325°F), Gas Mark 3. Line a baking tray (sheet) with nonstick baking paper.

6. Remove the dough from the refrigerator and shape into 60g balls. Place, evenly spaced, on the lined tray.

7. Bake for 15 minutes, then leave to cool on the tray.

Peanut Butter & Cardamom Cookies

INGREDIENTS

400g	butter
200g	caster (superfine) sugar
40g	light soft brown sugar
160g	crunchy peanut butter
1	egg, beaten
20g	fine sea salt
350g	plain (all-purpose) flour
200g	wholemeal flour
16g	ground cardamom seeds
½ tsp	bicarbonate of soda (baking soda)
150g	unsalted peanuts

METHOD

1. Cream the butter and both the sugars together in the bowl of a stand mixer fitted with a paddle attachment until the mixture is starting to turn pale and creamy, scraping down the sides of the bowl as needed.

2. Add the peanut butter and mix to combine. With the mixer running on low speed, drizzle in the egg and mix until combined.

3. In a clean bowl, mix together all the remaining ingredients, except the peanuts, then add half of the mixture to the mixer.

4. Turn the mixer to low speed and mix for about 15 seconds. Add the remaining flour mixture and mix for 15–30 seconds until a dough forms around the paddle.

5. As soon as a dough comes together, turn off the mixer so the dough isn't over worked. Turn the mixture out on to a large piece of baking paper and put another piece of paper the same size on top.

6. Press down with your hand to flatten the mixture out until it is 2cm (¾ inch) thick.

7. Using a rolling pin, roll out the mixture, between the baking papers, to a thickness of about 5mm (¼ inch).

(continued)

8. Carefully peel back the top layer of paper and sprinkle the peanuts evenly over the top.

9. Cover again with the baking paper and gently roll the rolling pin over the top to push the peanuts down into the dough.

10. Chill the dough in the refrigerator for about 30 minutes (or up to 24 hours).

11. Preheat the oven to 170°C (335°F), Gas Mark 3 and line a baking tray (sheet) with nonstick baking paper.

12. Once firm, remove from the refrigerator and carefully peel off the top piece of paper.

13. Using a knife or a pastry wheel cutter, cut the dough in into 5cm (2-inch) squares and arrange the squares on the lined tray, leaving a couple of centimetres (about an inch) between each, as they will grow a little in the oven.

14. Bake in the oven for 14–16 minutes until the cookies are golden brown, starting to crack on the surface and feel firm when pressed lightly with your fingertip. As the cookies cool, they will harden up and should have a nice crunch and snap when ready.

Baneta Yelda
CAMPANIO BAKERY

Makes
15 COOKIES

Pistachio & Rosewater Cookies

This recipe was inspired by the biscuits (cookies) I made with my mother as a kid; pistachio goes in almost every dessert we make in our home and I added almonds to the recipe after I travelled to Italy to see my parents while I was a refugee, the only family reunion we had in seven years.

INGREDIENTS

100g	egg whites (about 3 eggs)
250g	caster (superfine) sugar, plus 40g for rolling the biscuits before baking
30g icing (confectioners') sugar	
180g	ground almonds
5g	rosewater
3g	vanilla extract
100g	chopped pistachios (I keep them coarse for nicer texture)

METHOD

1. Preheat the oven to 160°C (325°C), Gas Mark 3, and line a baking tray (sheet) with nonstick baking paper.

2. Place the egg whites in a bowl and whisk till foamy; you can use a stand mixer on medium speed if you are feeling lazy like me.

3. Put the 40g of caster (superfine) sugar and the icing (confectioners') sugar on separate plates and put to the side.

4. Put the ground almonds, chopped pistachios and the 250g of caster (superfine) sugar in a bowl. Gently fold in the beaten egg whites, then add the rosewater and vanilla extract and keep folding until smooth.

5. Divide the mix into 40g balls if you have a scale; if not, the mix makes 15 biscuits (cookies). Roll them in the caster (superfine) sugar first, then coat them with the icing (confectioners') sugar.

6. Place on the lined tray with 2.5cm (1 inch) between the balls. Place in the oven and bake for 15–18 minutes.

7. Leave them to cool for a few minutes then move to a wire rack to cool. They always taste the best when shared!

Chocolate Chip Cookies

INGREDIENTS

180g	butter, at room temperature
255g	caster (superfine) sugar
2	eggs
4g	vanilla extract
255g	plain (all-purpose) flour
3g	baking powder
4g	fine salt
220g	dark (semisweet) chocolate chips

METHOD

1. Preheat the oven to 200°C (400°F), Gas Mark 6. Line a baking tray (sheet) with nonstick baking paper.

2. In the bowl of a stand mixer, cream the butter and sugar together until light and fluffy, then slowly add the eggs with the machine running.

3. Stop the machine, add the vanilla and all the dry ingredients (flour, baking powder and salt) and mix until just combined, then add the chocolate chips and mix to just combine.

4. Scoop the mixture into approx. 85g balls and place on the lined tray. Leave enough space between the balls for the cookies to expand as they cook.

5. Bake for 15 minutes then leave to cool on the tray.

Pumpkin Spice Snickerdoodles

Snickerdoodles are hard not to love at any time of the year: they're slightly cakey in the centre, crisp at the edges, cracked on top and rolled in cinnamon sugar; they're also great as the base for an ice-cream sandwich. Here, I've given them an autumnal, pumpkin spice twist. The cookies keep in a sealed jar for up to a week, and can also be baked straight from frozen, in which case add 1 minute to the baking time.

INGREDIENTS

PUMPKIN SPICE MIX

4 tsp	ground cinnamon
2 tsp	ground ginger
¼ tsp	ground cloves
1 tsp	ground nutmeg
50g	demerara (turbinado) sugar

SNICKERDOODLE DOUGH

340g	plain (all-purpose) flour
1 tsp	bicarbonate of soda (baking soda)
1 tsp	cream of tartar
250g	unsalted butter, at room temperature
300g	caster (superfine) sugar
½ tsp	sea salt flakes
1 tsp	vanilla bean paste
1	egg, lightly beaten

METHOD

1. First make the pumpkin spice mix. Put the cinnamon, ginger, cloves and nutmeg in a small bowl. Spoon 2 teaspoons of the mix into a large bowl, add the flour, bicarb (soda) and cream of tartar and set aside. Add the sugar to the remaining spice mix in the small bowl and set that aside, too.

2. Now for the dough. Put the butter, sugar and salt in the bowl of a stand mixer fitted with the paddle attachment. Mix on a medium–high speed for 10 minutes, until light and fluffy. Add the vanilla and egg, and continue mixing on a medium–high speed for 1 minute until everything is well incorporated.

3. With the motor running, add the flour mixture in 3 batches, scraping down the sides of the bowl as you go. Scrape the dough to the bottom of the bowl, making sure there are no bits stuck to the sides, then cover and refrigerate for 1 hour, until firm and rollable.

4. Preheat the oven to 200°C (400°F), Gas Mark 6. Line a large baking tray (sheet) with nonstick baking paper.

5. Divide the dough into 40g pieces and roll into firm balls: you should end up with 22. One at a time, roll the balls in the spice and sugar mixture, to coat well. (If it doesn't stick, warm the balls slightly in your hands first.)

6. Lay the balls on the lined tray (sheet), spacing them out well apart – they will spread a lot while baking, so leave at least 5cm (2 inches) between each ball, and if need be, use 2 trays and/or bake them in batches.

7. Bake for 9 minutes for a gooier cookie and up to 12 minutes for a firmer one, then remove, transfer to a wire rack to cool and serve warm or at room temperature.

Dominic Maciocia
WILLIAMS & JOHNSON COFFEE CO.

Makes
34 COOKIES

Cardamom, Rye & Chocolate Chip Cookies

INGREDIENTS

500g	butter
600g	wild-farmed flour
10g	ground cardamon
200g	dark rye flour
10g	baking powder
10g	bicarbonate of soda (baking soda)
10g	fine sea salt
4	eggs
500g	soft light brown sugar
140g	caster (superfine) sugar
1 tsp	vanilla extract
300g	dark (semisweet) chocolate chips
300g	white chocolate chips

sea salt flakes

METHOD

1. Preheat the oven to 160°C (325°C), Gas Mark 3. Line a baking tray (sheet) with nonstick baking paper.

2. In a saucepan, melt the butter and then remove from the heat.

3. Thoroughly mix the dry ingredients (the flour to the salt).

4. In the bowl of a stand mixer, whisk the eggs and sugars on fast speed for 10 minutes.

5. Slowly add the melted butter to the stand mixer, then the vanilla, then remove from the mixer and incorporate the dry mix slowly with spatula.

6. Add both the chocolate chips to the mixture, then divide into 80g pieces and place on the lined tray (sheet), spacing them apart as they will spread when they cook.

7. Top with a little sea salt and bake for 10–15 minutes.

TIP: The cookies should be a little underbaked as they will cook further on the tray. You can open the oven door halfway and pat them with the back of a tablespoon to make them spread out so they have a more even thickness.

Alix André
ARÔME BAKERY

Makes
23 SABLÉ BISCUITS (COOKIES)

Sesame Kinako Sablé

INGREDIENTS

95g	icing (confectioners') sugar
210g	unsalted butter
15g	egg yolk
260g	plain (all-purpose) flour
30g	kinako powder
10g	black sesame seeds
10g	white sesame seeds
200g	vanilla sugar
2	egg, beaten for eggwash

METHOD

1. In the bowl of a stand mixer fitted with the paddle attachment, mix the icing (confectioners') sugar and butter on a slow speed until well combined.

2. While the machine is running, slowly add the egg yolk and then add the flour, kinako powder and both sesame seeds to the mix.

3. Continue mixing on a slow speed until well combined. Remove from the bowl and shape into a tube shape approx. 4cm (1½ inches) in diameter. Wrap in nonstick baking paper and chill in the refrigerator overnight.

4. The next day, preheat the oven to 180°C (350°C), Gas Mark 4. Line 2 baking trays (sheets) with nonstick baking paper.

5. Remove the biscuit mix from the refrigerator and unwrap the dough. Place the vanilla sugar in a large mixing bowl. Brush the dough all over with beaten egg and roll in the vanilla sugar, then slice into 30g pieces.

6. Place on the lined trays with spaces in between and bake for 24 minutes.

TARTS / PIES

Tom Aikens
MUSE

Makes
1 LARGE TART

Tarte Tropézienne

INGREDIENTS

STARTER

60g	full-fat (whole) milk
25g	caster (superfine) sugar
2g	fast-action (active) dried yeast
170g	plain (all-purpose) flour
2	eggs, at room temperature

DOUGH

340g	plain (all-purpose) flour
50g	sugar
10g	fast-action (active) dried yeast
8g	salt
4	cold eggs
100g	butter, softened

oil, for greasing

2	egg yolks, beaten, for eggwash

TOPPING

50g	lightly salted butter, softened
50g	soft light brown sugar
50g	ground almonds
50g	strong flour
50g	pearl sugar

ORANGE BLOSSOM SYRUP

280g	sugar syrup
50g	orange blossom water
30g	kirsch
2	vanilla pods (beans), seeds scraped

PASTRY CREAM

500ml	full-fat (whole) milk
1	vanilla pod (bean), seeds scraped
6	egg yolks
80g	sugar
90g	plain (all-purpose) flour
15g	cornflour (cornstarch)
20ml	vanilla extract

CREME MOUSSELINE

500g	whipped double (heavy) cream
½	vanilla pod (bean), seeds scraped
100g	icing (confectioners') sugar, sifted

zest of 1 lemon

ASSEMBLY

10g dehydrated strawberry, crushed
10g dehydrated raspberry, crushed
100g fresh strawberries, sliced
100g fresh raspberries

METHOD

1. Stir all of the starter ingredients together with a spatula until the mixture is the consistency of a thick batter and smooth; this is your sponge.

2. Use it right away or, for best flavour, make it a day ahead of time: let it ferment for 1 hour at room temperature, then refrigerate it overnight. When you're ready to prepare

(continued)

your dough, scrape it into the bowl of your mixer.

3. For the dough, whisk together the flour, sugar, yeast and salt. Sprinkle this all over the sponge in the bowl of a stand mixer, and let it sit for 2 hours, 2½–3 if the sponge was refrigerated. The dome of the dry mix will crack as the sponge expands, which is a sign that the proving has started.

4. Add the cold eggs. Using the dough hook, beat the mixture for 2–3 minutes on medium speed. With the machine running, add the butter in small pieces at a time, letting the dough absorb each addition before adding another, about 2 minutes of mixing per tablespoon of butter. Notice how light and sticky the dough gets. Keep kneading the dough for 10 minutes to develop more structure and gluten.

5. Once the dough is uniform (it might take an extra bowl scraping or two), scrape it into an oiled bowl or rising container. Let it rise for another 1½ hours until it looks light and fluffy. Deflate the dough by gently pressing down on it with your hand to knock it back.

6. Make the topping: in the bowl of the stand mixer, add the softened butter, brown sugar, ground almonds and flour. Using the dough hook, knead this together until the consistency is coarse and grainy. Take out of the bowl, add the pearl sugar with your fingers, then set aside.

7. Roll the finished dough out to a thickness of about 1cm (½ inch), then trim it into a roughly 20cm (8-inch) diameter disc. Line a baking tray (sheet) with nonstick baking paper. Put the disc on the paper and brush well with eggwash, leaving a 2cm (¾-inch) ring to keep its shape as it rises. Allow it to rise for about 1–1½ hours until puffy.

8. Preheat the oven to 185°C (365°F), Gas Mark 4.

9. When the brioche has risen, brush it again with eggwash. Sprinkle the glazed surface with the topping mixture, then bake it for 15–20 minutes until golden. Allow it to cool completely before using.

10. Bring all orange blossom syrup ingredients to a simmer in a pan, then chill.

11. For the pastry cream: infuse the milk with the vanilla pods (beans) to 75°C (167°F) and leave for 30 minutes. Whisk together the egg yolks and caster (superfine) sugar till pale, then add the flour and cornflour (cornstarch). Whisk well and then pour in the milk. Mix well and then return to the pan to cook out. Stir well and bring to a simmer. Make sure that it's cooked out and then pass through a fine sieve.

12. For the crème mousseline: beat the pastry cream until smooth and then whisk the cream with the vanilla and icing (confectioners') sugar till thick. Fold the cream into the pastry cream, adding the lemon zest and half of the dehydrated raspberries and strawberries, making sure that it is thick. Place in a piping (pastry) bag fitted with a large star nozzle.

13. When the brioche has cooled down, slice in half crosswise with a serrated knife. Set the top half of the brioche aside, brush both sides with the syrup, then cover the base of the brioche with the crème mousseline: starting on the edge, pipe in a spiral motion, working inward.

14. When the base is completely covered, place the fresh fruit on top, and then the other half of the brioche, positioning it gently. Press the remaining crushed dehydrated raspberries and strawberries through a sieve onto the top as it is served.

Julia Bell
TEN BELLES

Makes
1 GALETTE

Wholewheat Rhubarb Galette

INGREDIENTS

GALETTE DOUGH

145g	cold butter
200g	wholemeal flour
4g	salt
12g	soft light brown sugar
25g	cold water
8g	cider vinegar
1	egg, beaten, for eggwash

RHUBARB COMPOTE

250g	rhubarb, cut into small pieces
25g	caster (superfine) sugar

RHUBARB TOPPING

50g	caster (superfine) sugar
5g	ground cardamom
450g	rhubarb
pinch of sea salt	

METHOD

1. Rub together the butter and all the dry dough ingredients to form a sandy texture while retaining small lumps of butter. Slowly add the water and cider vinegar and mix until the dough is just combined.

2. Roll into a 30cm (12-inch) circle, 3mm (1/8 inch) thick. Rest in the refrigerator, covered with a tea towel, for 30 minutes.

3. Toss the rhubarb compote ingredients together and cook in a pot over a medium heat until the rhubarb has released its water. Lower the heat and cook out until the rhubarb has fallen apart and the mixture has thickened. Set aside to cool.

4. Preheat the oven to 180°C (350°C), Gas Mark 4 and line a baking tray (sheet) with nonstick baking paper.

5. For the rhubarb topping, mix together the sugar and cardamom in a bowl. Freshly cut the rhubarb into 4cm (1½-inch) pieces and mix with ¼ of the sugar mixture. Reserve the rest for finishing the galette.

6. Place the galette dough on the lined tray (sheet) and allow to warm up slightly. Spread the cooled compote in an even layer on the pastry, leaving a 3cm (1¼-inch) gap around the edge.

(continued)

7. Arrange the cut rhubarb on top, starting from the upper left of the compote: 1 piece horizontally followed by 1 piece vertically until the compote is covered in parquet floor style.

8. Gently fold the pastry over the edges of the rhubarb, pressing firmly to seal the pastry in place.

9. Brush the crust lightly with eggwash and sprinkle it with a little of the cardamom sugar. Sprinkle the remaining sugar mix and a pinch of sea salt over the rhubarb.

10. Bake in the oven for 30 minutes.

11. Remove from the oven and allow to cool before slicing into 6 or 8 pieces and serving plain or with a dollop of crème fraîche.

Nicola Lamb
LARK!

Makes
I PIE

Pear & Caramel Pie

Before we begin… For this recipe, you just need to BRING the confidence. The faster you work, the better your dough will be, as the butter won't have a chance to melt, so just bloody go for it. Leave the butter in bigger chunks than you think, because we'll be doing a folding method to keep it flaky. And remember, you've got this!

INGREDIENTS

PIE DOUGH

60g	cold water
60g	crème fraîche or soured cream
280g	plain (all-purpose) flour, plus extra if needed
6g	salt
25g	caster (superfine) sugar
225g	butter, cut into small cubes

PEARS

1.3kg	pears
20g	lemon juice
100g	dark brown sugar
I	vanilla pod (bean), split and seeds scraped

CARAMEL SAUCE

100g	caster (superfine) sugar
60g	double (heavy) cream
45g	butter
I–2g	salt, to taste

FOR ASSEMBLING

40g	plain (all-purpose) flour
2	eggs, beaten, for eggwash
demerara (turbinado) sugar	

METHOD

PIE DOUGH

1. Whisk the water and crème fraîche/soured cream/buttermilk together and set aside in the refrigerator or freezer to chill.

2. Mix together the flour, salt and sugar and whisk to evenly distribute everything.

3. Add the butter cubes into the flour and toss to coat. Coating the flour will help protect it from the warmth of your hands to stop it getting melty and thus negatively impacting the flake-factor of your pie dough.

4. Squish the butter into flat pieces, one-by-one. Now it's time to add the chilled liquid – pour in half and toss the bowl so the liquid is distributed evenly around the dry ingredients. Now add the rest and squish together. As soon as it doesn't feel like total desolation, tip the dough on to a work surface.

5. Squash everything together as best you can and then, adding flour if you need, roll out the dough then perform a single turn. This means folding the dough like a business letter, bringing

(continued)

the top third into the middle, and the bottom third over the middle. You'll see chunks of butter turn into long thin pieces – it's quite satisfying!

6. Press the dough back together – adding more flour if you need – then perform 2 more single turns until the dough is homogeneous but you can see big, lovely marble-y streaks of butter. Divide the dough into chunks at this stage – squares are fine, we'll roll it out later – wrap with a tea towel and put into the refrigerator for 1½ hours (minimum) for it to firm back up.

7. To roll it out, flour your surface enough to stop any dough sticking, then roll the pie dough out to 3mm (⅛-inch) thick. This is way thinner than you think is going to work. Trust me. I've made a lot of pie doughs that are TOO THICK because I simply haven't *trusted the process*, but you do want to go quite thin here. You'll still get a fantastic chubby edge as you fold the dough on itself anyway during lining, so don't worry about losing any drama.

8. If the dough is warming up too much and it doesn't feel cute… just put it in the refrigerator and return to it in 10 minutes. For this pie, you'll need to roll out both the top and bottom crust. You can do this in advance and put into the refrigerator, as long as you wrap it really well, okay!

PEARS

1. Peel the pears and remove the insides. I have a melon baller tool that is super useful for this job.

2. Cut into irregular-sized chunks and toss in the lemon juice. I like doing this because it is more interesting to eat. You should have about 1kg pear chunks.

3. Add to a saucepan with the dark brown sugar and vanilla pod (bean). Cook on a low–medium heat until the pears have taken on a caramel colour (looks like potatoes in gravy, okay) and are slightly soft. Don't go too far, just until they are gently cooked and not falling apart.

4. Drain the pears, reserving the liquid. You should have around 800g pears and 200g liquid. Reduce the liquid in a small pan on a medium heat until you have about 150g liquid. If you can't be bothered to do this, you can just use 150g of the un-reduced liquid and discard/eat/use elsewhere the other 50g. Allow both the pears and liquid to cool. You can do this step in advance! Up to 3 days in advance, in fact.

CARAMEL SAUCE

1. Heat the sugar in a pan over a medium heat until totally melted. You can move it around with a silicone spatula if you like, but we aren't making a large batch so you shouldn't need to. Once it's melted, watch it – you want it to be dark. Be brave!

2. Whisk in the cream, which will bubble aggressively, followed by the butter and salt. Leave to cool. It will firm up so you might need to rewarm it for this recipe to make it usable.

ASSEMBLING THE PIE

1. Whisk 150g of the pear liquid into 110g of the caramel sauce. Into this, whisk your sifted flour until its totally dissolved. Finally mix this liquid up with all the pears in a big bowl.

2. Line your pie dish (I use a dish that is approximately 20cm (8-inches) wide and 5cm (2-inches) deep) with your 3mm (⅛-in)-thick pie dough. Make sure it is nicely nestled into the edges and leave 2–3cm (¾–1¼ inches) overhang.

3. Pile in ALL the filling. I know, it looks dangerously full. Just go for it. Be brave. Place the top crust on top and press both bits of overhang together. Squish them a bit if you need to – just try and get a decent seal.

4. Move the pastry up-and-in on itself to create a crust and lock in the fruit, then when you're satisfied, trim the edges of the pressed dough so you have about 2cm (¾ inch) overhang. Tuck the dough under itself o create a crust, then crimp it using two fingers. Chill the pie in the freezer for 15 minutes. Preheat the oven to 220°C (425°F), Gas Mark 7.

5. When the pie is chilled, eggwash (go hard on the top, but less hard on the edges as these bits tend to stick out and brown easily anyway), generously add demerara (turbinado) sugar, then stab some holes into the top.

6. Turn the oven down to 205°C (400°F), Gas Mark 6. Put the pie on a baking tray (sheet) – it will get buttery! – and then place in the oven.

7. Bake for 1 hour, turning after 40 minutes. At the 40-minute turning mark, if it's getting too dark, then reduce the temperature to 170°C (335°F), Gas Mark 3 for the rest of the baking time.

8. After the full hour, it should be golden and well baked. If yours is looking like it *could* take longer, then leave it in for a further 15–20 minutes. I think is quite hard to overbake this pie, because it's so juicy and caramelly inside, so don't worry. Allow to cool for at least 2 hours.

9. Once cool, you can pipe in your caramel sauce! This is best done just before serving.

Get about 50g of caramel sauce in a piping (pastry) bag, ideally with a doughnut bismark tip, then STAB YOUR PIE (the vents come in handy) and squeeze in caramel sauce for extra joy.

10. To rewarm, heat for about 15–20 minutes in a hot oven OR do it slice by slice.

Fritz Schoon
SCHOON

Makes
12 PASTRIES

Pastéis de Nata

INGREDIENTS

STOCK SYRUP

350g   caster (superfine) sugar
150ml   water
1   cinnamon stick
zest of 1 lemon

BASE DOUGH

140g   plain (all-purpose) flour, plus extra
        for dusting
3g   salt
80ml   water
135g   cold butter

CUSTARD

400ml   full-fat (whole) milk
40g   self-raising flour
20g   cornflour (cornstarch)
4   egg yolks

ground cinnamon, to decorate

METHOD

1. Start this process a few days before.
To make the stock syrup, combine all the
ingredients in a saucepan, place on the heat
and bring to the boil. Allow to simmer for
5–8 minutes and then remove from the heat
and leave to cool. Keep in the fridge until you
are ready to use.

2. Place the flour, salt and water in the bowl of
a stand mixer fitted with a dough hook. Mix on
medium speed until the dough is combined.

3. Shape the dough into a ball, cover with
clingwrap (plastic wrap) and place in the
refrigerator.

4. While the dough is resting in the
refrigerator, slice the cold butter into 5mm-
(¼-in)-thick slices (this is easier than pounding
the butter) and place back in the refrigerator.

5. Remove the dough and butter from the
refrigerator after 1 hour.

6. Place the dough on a lightly floured surface.
Roll the dough out into a rectangle using a
rolling pin. Place the butter slices in the centre
of the dough.

7. Fold the dough from the bottom over the
butter. Fold the dough from the top as well to
cover the butter. Dust lightly with flour. Turn
the dough clockwise 90 degrees.

(continued)

8. Roll out the dough with rolling pin into rectangle about 1cm (½ inch) thick. Fold the dough again from the top and from the bottom, crossing over each other. Turn the dough again clockwise 90 degrees. Dust lightly with flour.

9. Roll out the dough again into a rectangle about 1cm (½ inch) thick. Fold the dough once more from the top and from the bottom, crossing over.

10. Cover the dough with clingfilm (plastic wrap), then place in the refrigerator to rest for 30 minutes. Repeat this process of rolling out and folding a further 3 times.

11. Roll the dough out to 5mm (¼ inch). Then roll it up from one side into a cylinder shape. Cover with clingfilm and return to the refrigerator to cool down once more until ready to use. (The dough can also be frozen and used at a later stage.) The dough needs to be completely cold before cutting and moulding.

12. Cut the dough into 12 equal discs. (Or to be more specific, 30g each.) Spray a 12-hole cupcake tray (pan) with a releasing agent.

13. Place a disc at the bottom of each hole. Spread the dough equally up the sides of the tray using your thumbs.(Helpful tip: slightly wet the thumbs.) Do not tear the dough. Spread evenly to cover the entire indentation of the mould. It should be flush with the top of the mould.

14. Place the tray in the refrigerator.

15. Place a baking stone or baking tray (sheet) inside the oven and preheat the oven to 250°C (500°F), Gas Mark 10, or the highest temperature on the convection setting for at least 30 minutes while you make the custard.

CUSTARD

1. It is very important to have all the ingredients scaled and ready before starting the process, as you cannot leave your pot once you start. Mix the flour and cornflour together and pour 100ml of the milk into the flour mix, whisking until a smooth paste has formed.

2. Pour the remaining 300ml milk into a pot over a medium heat. Then pour the flour and milk mixture into the pot with the milk. Continue whisking (do not leave your pot) until the milk has thickened. It should be very thick with bubbles starting to appear as you whisk. Remove from the heat immediately.

3. Pour your stock syrup into the thickened milk and whisk thoroughly until it has completely combined.

4. Add the egg yolks to the milk-syrup mixture and whisk until combined. Pour your custard into a pouring jug. Take your moulded dough tray out of the refrigerator and pour equal amounts of custard into each mould.

BAKING AND FINISHING

1. Carefully place the cupcake tray in the oven on the hot stone/tray and quickly close the door. Bake for 18 minutes.

2. Remove from the oven. Allow to cool and remove from the moulds with a palette knife.

3. Sprinkle the pastries with a little ground cinnamon to finish.

Asa Balanoff Naiditch
BLAME BUTTER

Makes
1 PIE

Peanut Butter Banana Cream Pie

INGREDIENTS

CRUMB CRUST

200g	digestive biscuits (Graham Crackers) or Biscoff biscuits (cookies)
30g	granulated sugar
2g	salt
80g	butter, melted

PB BANANA PUDDING

150g	banana, for the pudding, plus 1 banana to line the pie
squeeze of lemon	
345g	full-fat (whole) milk
230g	whipping cream
180g	creamy peanut butter (not natural)
75g	granulated sugar
75g	dark brown sugar (if you only have light brown sugar, that's fine too)
30g	cornflour (cornstarch)
3g	salt
5	egg yolks
30g	butter

CLASSIC WHIPPED CREAM

350g	whipping cream
40g	icing (confectioners') sugar
3g	vanilla extract

METHOD

CRUMB CRUST

1. Blitz the biscuits (or crackers) in a food processor until you have very fine crumbs, a sandy consistency. Pour the crumbs into a bowl, add the sugar and salt, and mix. Add the melted butter and mix with a fork until it has been evenly incorporated.

2. Pour the crumbs into a 23cm (9-inch) pie dish and press the crust evenly up the sides of the dish and evenly over the base. Make sure all the crumb is pressed in and you have an even layer. Transfer to the freezer while you prepare the filling.

PB BANANA PUDDING

1. Lightly smash the 150g bananas and add a small squeeze of lemon to stop them from browning. Set aside.

2. In a medium saucepan, heat the milk, cream and peanut butter until the peanut butter has melted and the mixture is steaming. Stir occasionally to help incorporate the peanut butter.

3. While the milk mixture heats, whisk the sugars, cornflour (cornstarch) and salt together in large bowl until combined.

(continued)

4. Add the egg yolks all at once to the sugar, cornflour (cornstarch) and salt, and whisk the mixture well until it turns into a paste.

5. Once the milk and peanut butter mixture is steaming, slowly whisk half into the egg-sugar paste to temper the eggs. Pour the egg mixture back into the saucepan, whisking constantly until it boils large bubbles and thickens.

6. Remove from the heat and stir in the butter. Strain through a fine-mesh sieve if there are any lumps. Add the smashed bananas and mix until combined.

7. Take the crust from the freezer, slice the single banana and line the entire pie crust base with the slices, even going up the sides.

8. Pour the hot peanut butter filling into the pie crust and smooth into an even layer. Cover the pie with clingfilm (plastic wrap) pressed against the surface to prevent a skin from forming. Refrigerate for a minimum of 3 hours until fully set and cooled.

CLASSIC WHIPPED CREAM

1. In the bowl of a stand mixer fitted with the whisk attachment, combine the cream, sugar and vanilla and beat on medium–high speed until the cream is voluminous, smooth and holds its shape (medium peaks).

2. Spoon the whipped cream on top of the chilled pie. Add shards of peanut brittle if using and serve.

OPTIONAL: PEANUT BRITTLE
(for a dramatic look)

INGREDIENTS

100g	granulated sugar
57g	water
58g	butter
35g	light corn syrup
½ tsp	bicarbonate of soda (baking soda)
85g	roasted, salted peanuts
sea salt flakes, for sprinkling	

METHOD

1. Line a baking tray (sheet) with nonstick baking paper.

2. In a small pot, combine the sugar, water, butter and light corn syrup.

3. Bring to a boil (148°C/298°F), stirring occasionally. Take off the heat and stir in the bicarbonate of soda (baking soda), followed by the nuts.

4. Pour on to the lined tray and spread evenly. Sprinkle with salt. Leave to cool completely (about 30 minutes) before breaking into shards.

Strawberry & Almond Tart

INGREDIENTS

SWEET PASTRY

175g	plain (all-purpose) flour
½ tsp	fine sea salt
110g	unsalted cold butter
50g	icing (confectioners') sugar
30g	egg yolks

FILLING

350g	unsalted butter
350g	caster (superfine) sugar
350g	almonds
3	eggs

TO SERVE

800g	seasonal strawberries

icing (confectioners') sugar, for dusting

METHOD

1. For the sweet pastry, pulse the flour, salt and butter in a food processor until the mixture resembles coarse breadcrumbs.

2. Add the sugar, then the egg yolks and pulse. The mixture will immediately combine and leave the sides of the bowl.

3. Remove, wrap in clingfilm (plastic wrap), and chill in the refrigerator for at least 1 hour.

4. Preheat the oven to 160°C (325°C), Gas Mark 3.

5. Coarsely grate the pastry into a 30cm (12-inch) loose-bottomed fluted flan tin, then press it evenly on to the sides and base.

6. Bake blind for 16 minutes until very light brown. Leave to cool.

7. Reduce the temperature to 150°C (300°F), Gas Mark 2.

8. For the filling, cream the butter and sugar until the mixture is pale and light. Put the almonds in a food processor and chop until fine. Add the butter and sugar and blend, then beat in the eggs one-by-one. Pour into the pastry case and bake for 90 minutes.

9. Cool, cover with strawberries and dust with icing (confectioners') sugar before serving.

CONTRIBUTORS

Tom Aikens, Muse, London

Tom Aikens is one of the UK's most acclaimed and inspirational chefs. Growing up in Norfolk, Tom spent his childhood gardening and cooking with his mother, learning how to make use of the freshest ingredients, putting food at the centre of his life from a very early age. Tom became the youngest British chef ever to be awarded two Michelin stars, aged just 26, a record he still holds to this day.

Alix André, Arôme, London

French techniques are the cornerstone of Arôme, but its menu extends far beyond, drawing inspiration from Singapore and Japan as well. This unique fusion is on display at 9 Mercer Street in London's Covent Garden. The bakery's interior focuses on simplicity and functionality, with an East Asian-inspired room; the menu, meanwhile, offers elegant pastries, breads and desserts such as Honey Butter Toast and Miso Bacon Escargot. Heading up the operation are co-founders French-born pâtissier Alix André and Singaporean restaurateur Ellen Chew.

Ixta Belfrage, Chef

Ixta's style of cooking draws inspiration from three countries: Brazil (where her mother is from), Italy (where she lived as a child) and Mexico (where her grandfather lived). She cut her teeth at Yotam Ottolenghi's NOPI restaurant before moving to the Ottolenghi Test Kitchen, where she worked for Yotam Ottolenghi for five years, contributing to his columns in *The Guardian* and *The New York Times*. In 2020 she co-authored *The New York*

Times best-selling *Ottolenghi Flavour* and in 2021 she was named one of the most influential women in food by Code Hospitality.

Julia Bell, Ten Belles, Paris

Originally from New Zealand, Julia worked in both Australia and Canada before relocating to Paris seven years ago. She grew up in a family of market gardeners, instilling in her a love of growing and using produce straight from the earth. As a pastry chef she loves simple techniques and clean, balanced flavours that really elevate the produce and allow the ingredients to shine.

Richard Bertinet, The Bertinet Kitchen, Bath

Originally trained as a baker in Brittany, Richard Bertinet has been in England since 1988. He opened The Bertinet Kitchen Cookery School in Bath in 2005 and his classes attract customers from all over the world to come to learn to bake with him. Richard has written 6 books, which have attracted many accolades. His first book *Dough* was awarded the IACP Best Cookery Book of the Year 2006, has been translated into 15 languages and is sold worldwide. Richard founded The Bertinet Bakery in 2008, which he grew to be the UK's first national artisan bakery with a range of products stocked in Waitrose, before selling in 2019.

Max Blachman-Gentile, Tartine Bakery, Los Angeles

Max is currently the Director of Culinary Operations at Tartine Bakery. Previously, at The Standard Hotel in New York, he started a bread programme using locally sourced, freshly milled grain. He grew up in Oakland, California, and was indoctrinated in the Bay Area culture of sourdough bread from an early age.

Romina Bacchi Bonelli, Blackbird Café, Valencia

Born in Venezuela to an Italian family, Romina came to the UK to improve her English and studied Graphic Design at Bournemouth Arts University from 2009 to 2013. She then moved to Sydney, Australia (2013–2015), and Queenstown, New Zealand (2016) where she fell in love with specialty coffee, hospitality and baking. Before moving to Valencia to open Blackbird, she expanded her knowledge on baking while working in Rome for a year. Essentially, all the above represents what Blackbird is: the marriage of Romina's love for homemade bakery, travel and specialty coffee.

Nick Bramham, Quality Wines, London

Nick is Head Chef at Quality Wines in Farringdon, London, where he cooks regional Mediterranean food and always has a fun sandwich on the menu.

Wayne Caddy, Consultant

Wayne is a sourdough slinger from Yorkshire and has been baking for over three decades. His obsession with fermentation and flour has taken him in many directions around the globe. He competed for Great Britain in the Coupe du Monde and was the first baker from the UK to be selected for the prestigious Masters de la Boulangerie. His heart is in helping the next generation of bakers to flourish and to support the artisanal bread revolution with practical skills workshops in the UK and beyond.

Jo Clarke and Aaron Kossoff, Kossoffs, London

The first Kossoffs bakery was established in the 1920s by Wolf Kossoff, a Jewish refugee from Kyiv. He went on to open several bakeries across East London. Three generations later, his great grandson Aaron has carried on the family tradition with girlfriend Jo Clarke. While the bakery today specializes in sourdough and viennoiserie, Aaron has stayed close to his roots in *Knead Peace* with his Jewish Apple Cake. As per tradition, the cake is dairy-free, meaning it can be eaten alongside meat-based meals.

Sally Clarke, Clarke's, London

Sally grew up in Surrey and studied at Croydon College, followed by Le Cordon Bleu. She worked in Paris, London and California before opening Clarke's Restaurant in 1984. She went on to open a shop, a wholesale bakery, a production kitchen and the Corner Shop. She has published three books: *Sally Clarke's Book: Recipes from a Restaurant, Shop and Bakery*; *30 Ingredients*; and *First Put on Your Apron*. In 2009 she was awarded an MBE in the Queen's birthday honours list for services to the hospitality industry.

Angharad Conway and Lance Gardner, Tŷ Melin Bakery, Cardiff

Tŷ Melin Bakery in Cardiff is the brainchild of bakers Lance Gardner and Angharad Conway. Angharad began her career working for Rick Stein. She then attended The School of Artisan Food and worked for Hobbs House Bakery as an in-house pastry chef, and in France as a pastry chef in a 4-star hotel. Lance began his baking journey under the pupillage of master baker Richard Bertinet in Bath. He furthered his career by heading up Hart's Bakery in Bristol and then London's Harrods bakery in its refurbished food hall. He was a teacher at Bread Ahead in Borough Market.

Nelson Fartouce, Layla, London

Layla is a neighbourhood artisan bakery working with regeneratively farmed grains and with a focus on sourdough bread and pastries.

Layla's Head Baker, Nelson Fartouce, has created this chocolate hot cross bun recipe (see page 80), which is a take on the buns served in the bakery in the run up to Easter. Layla is delighted to be a part of the *Knead Peace Cookbook* alongside such a prestigious line-up, having been open in Ladbroke Grove for only just over a year. Most importantly, they are happy to play a small part in supporting Ukraine at such a crucial time.

David Gingell, Big Jo, London

Growing up in Cornwall, David has always been involved in food. Aged 19 he moved to London where he was lucky enough to work in some of the capital's best restaurants. In 2012 David met his business partner, Jeremie Cometto-Lingenheim. Two years later, they opened Primeur and then Westerns Laundry, both in London, Fitzroy in Cornwall, and their small family of bakeries, Jolene. He believes that the real skill of a chef is finding a few really good-quality ingredients that work well together and treating them with the respect they deserve.

Helen Goh, Author and Recipe Developer

Helen is a recipe developer and co-author of Ottolenghi's *Sweet*. Helen draws widely on Southeast Asian, Western and Middle Eastern influences in her cooking – and of course, her love of sweets (candies). She is also a baking columnist for the *Good Weekend Magazine* in *The Age* and *Sydney Morning Herald* newspapers in Australia.

Andrew Green, Knead Peace, Totnes, Devon

Andrew's passion for artisan baking began at a young age while baking bread with his parents. He also spent time with his grandfather who was General Manager of the Strand Palace hotel. He started his own career in London

at the RAC club and the City of London Club. Andrew completed work stages in various Michelin starred restaurants, then moved to South Africa for love and went on to help launch multiple establishments as head chef. Andrew has won the Hirsch's Italian Oven Appliances competition and Saigon Suzy was awarded Best Asian Restaurant in the National Restaurant awards.

Shuna Griffin, The Uprise Bakery, Bristol

Based in Stoke Bishop, Bristol, The Uprise Bakery is a hand-crafted, small-batch micro-bakery specializing in sourdough and viennoiserie. They deliver bread-making workshops and fresh bread to their area of Bristol. Everything is baked with stone-milled, sustainable-population wheat and organic flour.

Zack Hall, Clark Street, Los Angeles

Clark Street was founded in 2014 by Zack Hall from his apartment in West Hollywood. After spending the summer in his wife's hometown working in a wood-fired bakery in the Swedish countryside, Hall returned home to become a full-time bread baker. Starting out in his apartment on Clark Street, Hall's passion for bread-making grew. He first delivered to West Hollywood institution and butcher shop Lindy & Grundy, but word spread fast. In 2015 Hall took up shop in Grand Central Market in Downtown LA. Today, Clark Street has four locations in Los Angeles.

Richard Hart, Hart Bageri, Frederiksberg

Richard is a baker and owner of Hart Bageri in Frederiksberg, Copenhagen. Richard started his career as a chef, working through the ranks of fine-dining kitchens in London. He moved to California to work with Jeremy Fox. In San Francisco he fell deeply in love with sourdough bread and has since dedicated his life to baking the elusive perfect loaf (something he achieves occasionally, although the rest are pretty good). He learned his craft at Della Fattoria and later Tartine where he was head baker for seven years before starting his own bakery in Denmark.

Anna Higham, The River Café, London

Anna is a pastry chef and writer. Her ingredient-led, seasonal approach to desserts has seen her in senior roles at Lyles and Flor, as Head of Pastry, and most recently at The River Café as Executive Pastry Chef. Her debut cookbook, *The Last Bite,* was published in May 2022.

Michael James, Consultant and Author

Michael James is an accomplished chef and baker who grew up in Penzance before moving to London, where he met his wife, Pippa James, at restaurant Pied à Terre. They moved to Australia in 2004, opening the Tivoli Road Bakery in Melbourne in 2013. As co-founders of Grainz, they are committed to sustainability as active members of Melbourne's baking, grain-growing and milling community. He consults internationally and teaches. Their first book, *The Tivoli Road Baker*, was published in 2017. The savoury follow up book, *All Day Baking* was published in 2021.

Sarah Johnson, Spring, London

Sarah Johnson is a pastry chef, food writer and advocate for regenerative farming. Originally from California, she worked at Alice Water's acclaimed Chez Panisse Restaurant before moving to London to head the pastry kitchen at Spring. Today she oversees the pastry development at Spring and Heckfield Place while collaborating with biodynamic growers in the UK.

Lily Jones, Lily Vanilli, London

Self-taught, Lily Jones (aka Vanilli) started out in 2008 by creating an industry-leading brand, and now consults for brands in the UK and overseas. She is co-founder of the industry-leading YBF Awards and founder of the viral fundraising campaign #BakeForSyria. She is the author of three best-selling recipe books and has a bakery on London's Columbia Road. Her bespoke cake and canapé business is a huge celebrity favourite. She recently opened a second store in Tbilisi, Georgia, and launched afternoon tea at the Theatre Royal Drury Lane in London's West End.

Matthew Jones, Bread Ahead, London

Matthew began his working life as a chef before being increasingly drawn to patisserie and bread-making. In 2013 Matthew opened Bread Ahead at Borough Market, London. Its approach is simple: seasonal quality ingredients that speak for themselves. Bread Ahead believes that every bake it produces should look and taste exceptional, from the first bite to the last crumb. Bread Ahead opened its first baking school in 2014 and now teaches all manner of baking workshops, from half-day croissant classes to its most extensive three-day complete sourdough baking course.

Roxana Jullapat, Friends & Family, Los Angeles

Roxana, a Los Angeles native of Costa Rican and Thai descent, spent 20 years as a baker and pastry chef at some of Los Angeles' most celebrated restaurants, including Campanile, Bastide, Lucques and AOC, before opening Friends & Family bakery in 2017. Her first cookbook, *Mother Grains: Recipes for the Grain Revolution,* was published in April 2021. She bakes most days and is working on a second cookbook – a deeper dive into wholegrain baking. Her recipes can be found in *Epicurious,*

Bon Appetit, Food & Wine, The Washington Post, and *Fine Cooking.*

Vanessa Kimbell, The Sourdough School, Pitsford, Northamptonshire

Over 25 years ago, French-trained sourdough baker Vanessa recognized that the bread we eat every day has a powerful influence on our health. She pioneered an evidence-based approach, reframing the way we bake and eat bread as lifestyle medicine. The Sourdough School was founded to provide ground-breaking education, research and development programmes to support both gut and mental health.

Jordon Ezra King, Mob, London

Jordon Ezra King is a cook, recipe developer, food producer and host of the 'Eat-o-mology' podcast. Jordon's approach to food is simple, approachable and grounded in the roots of where it comes from. Having cooked his way through a host of kitchens around the world (including Brawn, Le Saint Europe, Burro e Salvia and Yard, to name a few), Jordon uses his platform to host shit-hot pop-ups and help his followers get more comfortable in the kitchen. All, of course, while educating them about the provenance of what they're eating.

Phil King, Pophams, London

Phil was inspired by a visit with Tartine Bakery's Fausto Echeverria to San Francisco to start his training as an artisan baker. On his return, Phil joined Pophams bakery where he was mentored by the founding head baker, Florin. Alongside this, Phil set up a supper club with a menu focusing on specialities from Italy. This concept was expanded to become the dinner offering at the Pophams restaurant in Hackney, for which Phil became the head chef. He is now Executive Chef at Pophams, where he leads a team of skilled bakers and chefs.

Anne Sofie Kuhr Brasen and Peter Jespersen, Simple Sourdough, Viborg, Denmark

Anne Sofie Kuhr Brasen has a degree in nutrition and health. She has been employed in the food industry for 10 years, with mostly social (food) activities and events aimed at children and young people. Peter Jespersen is a chef and primarily worked at fine-dining restaurants in Denmark before becoming a head chef at a boarding school, together with Anne Sofie. From autumn 2022, he will start working full-time as an artisan baker.

Nicola Lamb, lark!, London

Nicola is a pastry chef, recipe developer and author of 'Kitchen Projects', a weekly deep dive into the 'why' of baking. She trained in New York and London's top bakeries, including Dominique Ansel, Ottolenghi and Little Bread Pedlar, and shares her concepts to sell-out pastry events in London with her pop-up, lark!

Ben Lines, Gwyn's Bakery, Horsham, West Sussex

Ben is the owner and Head Baker at Gwyn's Bakery in Horsham, which specializes in sourdough bread and a range of pastries. The bakery is nut- and sesame-free, allowing more people to enjoy its products. It uses the highest-quality ingredients, including chocolate from Pump Street, butter from Ampersand Dairy and flour from Wessex Mill and other local farms. The bakery is a completely open-plan shop and production space, which allows the customer to see the whole process, from the shaping to the baking of the bread.

Ben Lippett, Mob, London

Ben is a cook, food writer, recipe developer and co-founder of Dr. Sting's Hot Honey. He spent years working at restaurants in the

UK, USA and Australia, before making the leap to food media. Today, he is one of Mob's most essential food producers, knocking out high-quality recipes that are divvied out to the masses. Ben has a passion for cooking food, eating food and teaching others how to master making food. He knows his way around the pans and brings a real sense of personality and finesse to every dish he creates.

Alex Lynn, Blood's Bakery, Sydney

Alex founded Blood's Bakery, a cult, underground Sydney-based micro-bakery producing small-batch, high-quality sourdough and pastries, where everything is made by hand. Alex is as passionate about quality ingredients as he is about baking bread; he works with growers and producers from all over New South Wales.

Campbell MacFarlane, Rackmaster, Wickford, Essex

Starting as a kitchen unit fabricator, Rackmaster founder Campbell MacFarlane (who has more than 40 years of experience with bespoke engineering work) noticed a gap in the market for bespoke bakery equipment. Since then, the company has supplied bakery equipment to a wide range of clients, from one-man bands, to those operating on a larger scale with a bigger workforce. With an ability to provide equipment on a range of scales, Rackmaster is large enough to offer a wide choice of equipment, but small enough to remember those personal touches.

Dominic Maciocia, Williams & Johnson Coffee Co., Edinburgh

Dominic has worked as a pastry chef since 2012. He worked at Edinburgh establishments Timberyard, Aizle and Ondine, and then in London at sketch and Fera at Claridge's, before going back to Edinburgh, where he became Head Baker in wholesale bakery Quay Commons and then Head Pastry Chef at International Hotel Edinburgh. He then returned to Timberyard where he prepared home meals when the pandemic struck. Dominic has since partnered with Williams & Johnson Coffee Co., opening a bakery supplying cafés with wild-farmed sourdough, sourdough pastries, small tarts and more.

Ben MacKinnon, e5 Bakehouse, London

The e5 Bakehouse began in the spring of 2010, when Ben MacKinnon returned home after taking a short course in the essentials of sourdough bread-making at The School of Artisan Food. He commissioned and built a clay oven in the corner of a railway arch that became home to a small group of bakers, all learning as they went along. Founded with an intense commitment to sustainability, e5 Bakehouse has since expanded, tunnelling left and then right into adjacent arches, adding a pastry department, flour mill, chocolate facility and deli shop to the mix.

Anna Makievska, The Bakehouse, Kyiv

Born in Crimea (now occupied by Russia) and raised in Dnipro, Anna built her career as part of a unique Goodwine project in Kyiv. Along with the team, she developed The Bakehouse bakery. Anna then decided to become a baker herself; she started to bake at home, took bread classes in London, and finally got her professional baker's diploma at San Francisco Baking Institute. Whole foods and sourdough bread are essential parts of her work. Anna, with her husband Valeriy, is raising two daughters; she dreams about writing a book one day and dedicating it to her family.

Marcelo Martins, Little Bread Pedlar, London

Marcelo Martins is best known for his traditional Italian natural ferment Panettone, developed as Head Baker at Little Bread Pedlar. Prior to this, Marcelo worked for Jamie Oliver at Fifteen Restaurant as their baker, where Jamie described Marcelo's bread as 'the best sourdough bread I've ever eaten'. And before this he worked as a Head Pastry Chef and Baker for St John Restaurant under Justin Gellatly. Marcelo's signature baking is inspired by his upbringing in Brazil.

Kate Marton, Hylsten Bakery, Buckfastleigh, Devon

Hylsten Bakery is a sourdough bakery and school committed to only using UK stoneground flours. The bakery was founded by Kate Marton and Megan Nash with the aim of producing the most delicious, nutritious and sustainability produced bread possible. The bakery and school is their way of contributing towards building a resilient local food system, supporting local growers and millers, and sharing their knowledge of sourdough baking with their community.

Megan McSharry, Marmadukes, Sheffield

After several years living and working in London, struggling to find job satisfaction, Megan decided to pursue her dream and enrolled at Le Cordon Bleu on the boulangerie course. This introduction to bread helped her to leave London and further her study of all things bread at The School of Artisan Food, where she was taught by the brilliant Wayne Caddy. She is now the head baker at Marmadukes in Sheffield, where she is lucky enough to bake bread every day alongside some fantastic bakers and friends.

Alice Mohan, Alice, Copenhagen

After several years of working in restaurants and cafés in her native Ireland, Alice first came to Copenhagen to intern at restaurant Noma in 2018. It was not long before she fell in love with the city's baking scene, and so decided to trade late restaurant nights for early bakery mornings. She started working at Juno the bakery in 2019 and later moved to Alice in 2020, where she has enjoyed making pastries, bread and ice cream ever since.

Kelly Nadjarian and Alexandre Bettler, Today Bread, London

In 2006 Alex started The Bread Workshops while studying at the Royal College of Art. Making sourdough breads from home while learning the craft in local bakeries, Alex started delivering his sourdough breads by bike to a small but growing group of local friends, cafés and Bread Club members. Soon forced to transform a room of his flat into a mini bakery, it became clear it was time to open a real bakery! This happened in 2016 when Today Bread opened its doors in Walthamstow Central, purveying organic breads and great coffees to the local community while retaining bike deliveries. Originally from France, Kelly learned from great chefs including Pierre Hermé and Jean Georges Vongerichten. At 21, she left Paris for London where she worked for more than 10 years for 5-star hotels, working in some of the most famous and prestigious restaurants. During the pandemic, she discovered Today Bread and fell in love with its atmosphere and ethos.

Asa Balanoff Naiditch, Blame Butter, London

Asa is the founder and CPO (Chief Pie Officer) of Blame Butter, a secret micro-bakery specializing in American pies and other scrumptious treats. A native Chicagoan,

Asa moved to London in 2018 to attend Le Cordon Bleu, where she received degrees in pastry and bread baking. She started Blame Butter in 2021 to bring Brits the sweet American pies they didn't know they were missing. When she's not baking, Asa travels the world, sampling every baked good along the way. She swears it's for research!

Yotam Ottolenghi, Ottolenghi, London

Yotam Ottolenghi is the restaurateur and chef patron of five London-based Ottolenghi delis, as well as the NOPI and ROVI restaurants. He is the author of nine best-selling cookery books, which have garnered many awards, including the National Book Award for *Ottolenghi Simple*, which was also selected as Best Book of the Year by *The New York Times*. Yotam has been a weekly columnist for *The Guardian* for over 15 years and is a regular contributor to *The New York Times Magazine*. Yotam lives in London with his family.

Sarit Packer and Itamar Srulovich, Honey & Co., London

Sarit Packer and Itamar Srulovich opened Honey & Co. in 2012, launching Honey & Smoke Grill House and Honey & Spice Food Store close after. They host a podcast, 'Honey & Co.: The Food Sessions', write a weekly recipe column in *FT Magazine*, and have published four cookbooks. Honey & Co. moved to its new home in Bloomsbury in June 2022.

Darren Purchese, Burch & Purchese Sweet Studio, Melbourne

Darren Purchese is the owner and creator behind Melbourne's Burch & Purchese Sweet Studio. Darren's sweet centrepieces are in demand at some of Australia's most prestigious events, The Australian F1 Grand Prix and The Melbourne Spring Racing Carnival have all enjoyed Darren's signature 'tubes' cakes

and desserts. Darren's customers, fans and prestigious client list are hooked on his unique and delicious list of creations as well as his charm and hospitality. Darren is an author of five cookbooks and is a regular on TV, most notably Masterchef Australia.

Dee Rettali, Fortitude Bakehouse, London

Dee was at the forefront of the organic food movement, having founded Patisserie Organic in 1998; her belief in preserving traditional crafts using time-honoured techniques, and sourcing simple, seasonal ingredients, has informed the way she cooks and bakes ever since. She opened Fortitude in London in 2018 and has amassed a loyal following. The bakery specializes in the unique process of sourdough cake making.

Kevan Roberts, Consultant

Early in his baking journey, Kevan spent a year in France before going on to open Time Bakery and The Yorkshire School of Baking and spending time in new product development for the likes of Marks & Spencer's and Waitrose. He spent three years as a senior teacher at Bread Ahead baking school and is the author of *Baking Sourdough*. In 2021, he led a team to create Chestnut Bakery in London, but the desire to teach lured him to the National Bakery School. In autumn 2022 Kevan began a new role as Head of Artisan Bread, tutoring at The School of Artisan Food.

Lotte Rodgers, Flori, York

Lotte learned to make her Swedish buns from a baker in Lisbon. She would visit his bakery daily, mesmerized, so one day he came over and shaped one in front of her and told her to be there at 7a.m. the next morning with her apron on. Lotte was the first there and the last to leave, and made her first cardamom bun and croissant that shift. Lotte and her team now make hundreds of these beautiful buns to fill the bakery counters at Flori. They may be Swedish buns, but that recipe came home with Lotte from Lisbon.

Ruth Rogers, The River Café, London

The River Café has become a world-renowned London landmark, opened by Ruth Rogers and Rose Gray in 1987. It offers Italian food and wines inspired by Italy's varied regions. The menu changes twice daily, reflecting the best seasonal ingredients available. Designed by the Richard Rogers Partnership, floor-to-ceiling windows run the length of the dining room, offering a beautiful view of the garden and River Thames beyond. The atmosphere is relaxed and buzzing, and the open kitchen with its wood-fired oven is a focal point. In fine weather the restaurant extends out on to the south-facing terrace and offers an outdoor dining experience unequalled in London. Tables are surrounded by the fruit trees, herbs, flowers, Italian salad leaves and vegetables of the River Café garden – some of which may find their way on to your plate. The River |Café has had a Michelin star since 1998.

Mette Marie Sarbo and Kathrine Rosamunde, H.U.G Bageri, Copenhagen

Mette Marie Sarbo is gluten intolerant and Kathrine Rosamunde has coeliac disease. Having both always loved baking, it was a disaster when they found out that gluten was not their way to go. But they do not give up easily, and so they started their gluten-free journey, and in 2014 they opened a very small gluten-free and organic bakery. They have grown since, and now have a 'real' bakery in Copenhagen, H.U.G Bageri.

Fritz Schoon, SCHOON, Stellenbosch

Following a short career as a quantity surveyor, Fritz worked on an apprenticeship with legendary master baker Markus Färbinger from Ile de Pain. Along with his wife, Chanelle, and his sister, Katryn, Fritz formed Schoon de Companje in 2014. In 2017 Chanelle and Fritz started SCHOON and soon got the attention of a fast-moving health food entity, the Real Foods Group. In 2018, SCHOON officially joined the group and today has nine cafés and an ever-expanding artisan bakery.

Jess Shadbolt and Clare de Boer, King, New York City

Jess Shadbolt and Clare de Boer met working on the line at The River Café in London. Along with their partner, Annie Shi, they opened King in New York in 2016 and received a review from *The New York Times* in 2018, before being awarded Best New Chefs by *Food & Wine*. With Shi, de Boer and Shadbolt opened their second restaurant, Jupiter, in 2022 in the iconic Rockefeller Center. *The King Cookbook* is due to be published in Autumn 2024.

Thomas Soccoja, Grands Moulins de Paris

Thomas is from Strasbourg, France, a beautiful region. He studied and travelled around France as a baker for eight years before moving to the UK. For the last 10 years, he has worked for a French miller, where he has met many great bakers from around the UK. Thomas believes that baking is all about sharing the knowledge, experience and passion from farmers, millers and bakers, and this is what it takes to create the best loaves.

Beesham Soogrim, Consultant

Beesham, known as 'Beesham the Baker', is an artisan sourdough baker based in Sweden. He started working as a chef at age 20 in his native Mauritius before travelling and working in India, South Africa and Norway. He was involved in the opening of two successful vegetarian restaurants in Oslo before moving to Sweden, where he has been based for the past 30 years. He has taught sourdough baking for almost 10 years and launched a successful online masterclass during the pandemic that people from 140 countries have joined.

Felicity Spector, Journalist and Home Cook

Felicity worked as an international TV news journalist for 33 years, beginning in Moscow and Eastern Europe covering the Velvet Revolution in Prague and the fall of the Soviet Union. She received a Fulbright scholarship to take a mid-career masters in US politics at Harvard, then specialized in American elections for many years after that. In her spare time, she goes to restaurants and bakes at home. She has loved making friends through Instagram and getting involved with brilliant campaigns like Cook for Ukraine.

Sophia Sutton-Jones, Sourdough Sophia, London

Sourdough Sophia was born out of a lockdown during the pandemic, in Crouch End, North London. Wife and husband team Sophia and Jesse Sutton-Jones supported the community by baking sourdough bread and other beautiful bakes in their dining room, and delivered it all by bike to those who were in need. Very quickly the community came to love them, and they came to love the community. They now have a real bakery space so that everyone can thrive on the most flavourful and delicious sourdough bread in the area!

Kitty Tait, The Orange Bakery, Watlington, Oxfordshire

Kitty and her dad Al live in Watlington, Oxfordshire and between them run the Orange Bakery. From uniquely flavoured sourdough (miso and sesame, fig and walnut) to huge piles of cinnamon buns and Marmite and cheese swirls, they sell out every day and

queues stretch down the street. Kitty set up the bakery when she was 14 after struggling with her mental health and finding therapy through making bread. She and her father published *Breadsong: How Baking Changed Our Lives* in April 2022.

Leila Tang, Pastry Chef

Leila Tang was born and raised in South East London. She graduated with a degree in Social Anthropology and Media from Goldsmiths University before pursuing a career as a pastry chef. As a British-born Chinese woman whose family lived through war, poverty and displacement, she finds inspiration in the foods, flavours and experiences that bring comfort, togetherness and empowerment inthe situations that we least expect.

Daisy Terry, Dusty Knuckle, London

The Dusty Knuckle started in 2014, in a shipping container, when childhood friends Max Tobias and Rebecca Oliver, later joined by Daisy Terry, quit their jobs and started selling bread. The Dusty Knuckle eventually moved from their shipping container to a permanent space in 2018, where it now employs young people from around London who have had a difficult upbringing and teaches them baking, social and employment skills.

Anca Tînc, Ille Brød, Oslo

Anca is a Romanian baker living and working in Oslo, Norway. After moving to the Lofoten Islands in 2014, looking for a new challenge in her life, she started baking by accident in a traditional Norwegian bakery in Å i Lofoten. She fell in love with the trade and decided that baking was her path. In 2018, after spending 4 years in Lofoten and baking with a wood-fired oven, she moved to Oslo. There she started working with Martin Fjeld at Ille Brød, developing her sourdough bread baking skills. Since 2019, she has been Head Baker of Ille Brød.

Greg Wade, Publican Quality Bread, Chicago

Greg is Head Baker at Publican Quality Bread. A graduate of the Illinois Institute of Art's Culinary Program, Wade started his career at Taxim in Wicker Park before joining Girl & the Goat in 2010 and then Izard's Little Goat in 2013. He received James Beard nominations for Outstanding Baker in 2017 and 2018 and won their national recognition for Outstanding Baker in 2019. Wade was a founding member of the Artisan Grain Collaborative and was featured in the documentary, *Sustainable: A Documentary on the Local Food Movement in America*.

Baneta Yelda, Companio Bakery, Manchester

Baneta came to Britain as a refugee fleeing Iraq in 2014 when the Islamic State (ISIS) were advancing across the region. Since changing her career from biomedical science to baking, she has tried to express her Assyrian heritage with food. She co-owns Companio Bakery in Manchester, which allows her to embrace her roots and open conversations about the history of her country, its regions, its ethnicities and its indigenous people. Baneta notes that her country is made up of so many ethnicities and religions that, now, food is the only common language.

Cindy Zurias, Baker and Consultant, 26 Degrees Ltd, London

Born in Venezuela, Cindy studied a degree in gastronomy and sought new challenges in London, working her way up through the ranks of the capital's best Michelin-starred restaurants. She became Head Baker of Little Bread Pedlar, managing one of the UK's largest artisan bakeries; and at the height of the pandemic, her techniques returned record profits while eliminating the night shift. Her dream now is working towards a new efficient, healthy and sustainable bakery built on these years of experience in high-calibre hospitality.

TEXT AND PICTURE CREDITS

TEXT CREDITS

7–9 © Knead Peace, 2022; **12–13** © E5 Bakehouse, 2022; **14–15** © Anne Sofie Kuhr Brasen & Peter Jespersen, 2022; **16–18** © Vanessa Kimbell, 2022; **19–21** © Hanna Makievska, 2016; **22–23** © Wayne Caddy, 2022; **24–26** © E5 Bakehouse, 2022; **27–29** © Kate Marton, 2022; **30** © Campbell MacFarlane, 2022; **32–33** © Beesham Soogrim, 2022; **34–35** © Daisy Terry, 2022; **37–39** © Sophia Handschuh, 2022; **40–41** © Hardie Grant UK, 2021; **42–44** © Anca Tînc, 2022; **45–47** © Richard Hart, 2022; **48–50** © Max Blachman-Gentile, 2022; **51** © Andrew Green, 2022; **52** © Shuna Griffin, The Uprise Bakery, 2022; **56–58** © Jordon King, 2022; **59–60** © Dee Rettali, 2022; **61–63** © Leila Tang, 2022; **64** © Nick Bramham, 2022; **66** © Kevan Roberts, 2022; **68–70** © Ben Lippett, 2022; **71–72** © Jess Shadbolt and Clare de Boer, 2022; **73** © Sally Clark, 2022; **76–78** © Blackbird VLC, 2018; **79** © Richard Bertinet, 2022; **80–82** © Layla Bakery, 2022; **83–84** © Alex Lynn, 2022; **85** © Marcelo Martins, 2022; **86–88** © Lotte Rogers, 2022; **89–90** © Cindy Zurias, 2022; **91–93** © Wade, 2022; **94–95** © Felicity Spector, 2022; **99–100** © helen@ottolenghi.co.uk, 2022; **101–103** © Jo Clarke & Aaron Kossoff, 2022; **104–105** © Kitty Tait, 2022; **107** © @hugbakery 2022; **108** © Ty Melin Bakery, 2022 ; **109** © Alice Mohan, 2022; **110–112** © W.W. NORTON AND CO., 2021; **113–114** © Ixta Belfrage, 2022; **116–117** © Megan McSharry, 2022; **119** © David Gingell, 2022; **120–121** © Sarah Johnson, 2022; **113–115** © Lily Jones, 2022; **126–128** © Burch & Purchese Sweet Studio, 2022; **129–131** From *Honey & Co: The Baking Book*, by Sarit Packer & Utamar Srulovich (Hachette, 2015); **132** © Anna Higham, 2022; **134** © Today Bread, 2022; **136–137** © Thomas Soccoja, 2022; **140–142** © Michael James, 2018; **143** © Ben Lines, 2022; **144–146** © Phil King, 2022; **147** © Baneta Yelda, 2022; **148** © Zack Hall, 2022; **150–151** © Yotam Ottolenghi, 23.06.22; **153** © Dominic Maciocia, 2022; **154** © Alix André, 2022; **159–160** © Tom Aikens, 2022; **161–162** © Julia Bell, 2022; **164–167** © Nicola Lamb, 2022; **168–170** © Fritz Shoon, 2022; **171–173** © Asa Balanoff Naiditch, 2022; **174** © The River Café, 2022; **176–186** © Knead Peace, 2022

PICTURE CREDITS

All images © Jessica Wang, 2022 unless otherwise indicated

All illustrations © Jessica Gully, @jessmotif, 2022

1 © Laura Edwards, from Vanessa Kimbell, *Food for Thought* (Kyle Books, 2015); **6** © Baranov Dmitriy, 2022; **8ac** Photograph by Elena Heatherwick, © Yotam Ottolenghi; **8ar** © Cindy Zurias, 2022; **8acl** © Sarah Worrall, 2022; **8accl** Mark Lord Photography, © Kitty Tait and Al Tait, *Breadsong* (Bloomsbury, 2022); **8acr** © David Malosh, 2022; **8bcl** © Michael James, 2022; **8bccl** © Lance Gardner, 2022; **8bccr** © Fritz Schoon, 2022 **8bcr** © Iona Kong, 2022 **8bl** © Lizzie Mayson, 2022; **8br** © Beesham Soogrim, 2022; **15** © Laura Edwards, from Vanessa Kimbell, *Food for Thought* (Kyle Books, 2015) **17** © Vanessa Kimbell, 2022; **20–21** © Valeriia Horovets, 2022; **23** © Sarah Worrall, 2022; **28–29** © John Hersey, 2022; **31** ©2022 Jamie Oliver Enterprises Ltd. Photographer: Zachary Costa; **33** © Beesham Soogrim, 2022; **43** © Alex Conu, 2022 ; **46** © Ditte Isager, 2021; **48** © David Malosh, 2022; **53** © Shuna Griffin, The Uprise Bakery, 2022; **62** © Leila Tang, 2022; **67** © Kevan Roberts, 2022; **69** © Rollo Scott, 2022; **72** © Paul Quitoriano, 2022; **77** © Maximiliano Braun, 2022; **84** © Alex Lynn, 2022; **87** © Nick Harbourne, 2022; **92** © Kelly Sandos, 2022; **105** Mark Lord Photography, © Kitty Tait and Al Tait, Breadsong (Bloomsbury, 2022); **106** © @hugbakery 2022; **111** © Kristin Teig, 2020; **117** © Rebecca Crofts, 2022; **127** © Patricia Niven, 2022; **135** © Today Bread, 2022; **137** © Thomas Soccoja, 2022; **141** © Michael James, 2022; **149** © Kassandra Mendieta, 2022; **151** Copyright Guardian News & Media Ltd 2022. Yotam Ottolenghi's pumpkin spice snickerdoodles. Photograph: Louise Hagger/The Guardian. Food styling: Emily Kydd. Prop styling: Jennifer Kay. Food assistant: Valeria Russo; **152** © Dominic Maciocia, 2022; **155** © Oscar Tan, 2021; **163** © Thibaut Divay-Cessieux, 2022; **169** © Fritz Schoon, 2022; **175** © Matthew Donaldson, 2022

INDEX

METRIC-IMPERIAL CONVERSION TABLE

WEIGHT

5 g	⅛ oz	175 g	6 oz	700 g	1 lb 9 oz
10 g	¼ oz	200 g	7 oz	750 g	1 lb 10 oz
15 g	½ oz	225 g	8 oz	800 g	1 lb 12 oz
25/30g	1 oz	250 g	9 oz	850 g	1 lb 14 oz
35 g	1¼ oz	275 g	9¾ oz	900 g	2 lb
40 g	1½ oz	280 g	10 oz	950 g	2 lb 2 oz
50 g	1¾ oz	300 g	10½ oz	1 kg	2 lb 4 oz
55 g	2 oz	325 g	11½ oz	1.25 kg	2 lb 12 oz
60 g	2¼ oz	350 g	12 oz	1.3 kg	3 lb
70 g	2½ oz	375 g	13 oz	1.5 kg	3 lb 5 oz
85 g	3 oz	400 g	14 oz	1.6 kg	3 lb 8 oz
90 g	3¼ oz	425 g	15 oz	1.8 kg	4 lb
100 g	3½ oz	450 g	1 lb	2 kg	4 lb 8 oz
115 g	4 oz	500 g	1 lb 2 oz	2.25 kg	5 lb
125 g	4½ oz	550 g	1 lb 4 oz	2.5 kg	5 lb 8 oz
140 g	5 oz	600 g	1 lb 5 oz	2.7 kg	6 lb
150 g	5½ oz	650 g	1 lb 7 oz	3 kg	6 lb 8 oz

VOLUME

1.25 ml	¼ tsp	150 ml	5 fl oz / ¼ pt	700 ml	1¼ pint
2.5 ml	½ tsp	175 ml	6 fl oz	850 ml	1½ pint
5 ml	1 tsp	200 ml	7 fl oz / 1/3 pt	1 litre	1¾ pint
10 ml	2 tsp	225 ml	8 fl oz	1.2 litres	2 pints
15 ml	1 tbsp / 3 tsp / ½ fl oz	250 ml	9 fl oz	1.3 litres	2¼ pints
30 ml	2 tbsp / 1 fl oz	300 ml	10 fl oz / ½ pt	1.4 litres	2½ pints
45 ml	3 tbsp	350 ml	12 fl oz	1.7 litres	3 pints
50 ml	2 fl oz	400 ml	14 fl oz	2 litres	3½ pints
60 ml	4 tbsp	425 ml	15 fl oz / ¾ pt	2.5 litres	4½ pints
75 ml	5 tbsp / 2½ fl oz	450 ml	16 fl oz	2.8 litres	5 pints
90 ml	6 tbsp	500 ml	18 fl oz	3 litres	5¼ pints
100 ml	3½ fl oz	568 ml	1 pint		
125 ml	4 fl oz	600 ml	20 fl oz		

THE UKRAINE HUMANITARIAN APPEAL OF THE DISASTERS EMERGENCY COMMITTEE

The Disasters Emergency Committee (DEC) brings together 15 leading aid charities to raise funds quickly and efficiently at times of crisis overseas. In these times of crisis, people in life-and-death situations need our help and our mission is to save, protect and rebuild lives through effective humanitarian response.

In February 2022 Russia invaded Ukraine. More than 6 million people have fled Ukraine and on top of this over 7 million have left their homes to escape the conflict, leading to a huge humanitarian crisis.

Heavy fighting, shelling and air strikes across the country have had devastating consequences for civilians. Homes have been destroyed. Families have been separated. Lives have been lost.

Millions of refugees have fled to Poland, Romania, Hungary and Moldova, often arriving with only what they could carry.

In Ukraine, those who are unable to leave due to age or disability have found themselves isolated, without access to food and basic necessities. DEC charities and their local partners are in Ukraine and in neighbouring countries providing food, water, shelter and medical assistance.